QUICK & EASY RÉSUMÉ MAKEOVERS

BOOST YOUR RÉSUMÉ AND COVER LETTER WITH KEY WORDS TO GET THE JOB IN 2017

Dawn Richards

info@smartstartmarketing.com.au

www.smartstartmarketingsolutions.com.au

www.getthatgovernmentjob.com

Dawn Richards

QUICK & EASY RÉSUMÉ MAKEOVERS

BOOST YOUR RÉSUMÉ AND COVER LETTER WITH KEY WORDS TO GET THE JOB IN 2017

Published in April 2017 in paperback format

The purchase of this publication entitles the purchaser to one copy of the publication.

First published in 2017 by Smart Start Marketing Solutions

The National Library of Australia Cataloguing-in-Publication data

Richards, Dawn

Quick & Easy Résumé Makeovers :

ISBN - 10: 0-9757245-3-3

ISBN – 13: 978-0-9757245-3-8

1. Applications for positions. 2. Résumés (Employment)

Title. 650.14 Designed by: Dawn Richards

Who will benefit from reading this book?

Applicants who have been sending off loads of applications, without getting a response, this book will show you the NEW WAY to write résumés for the NEW JOB MARKET in 2017.

Applicants who are in a contract position (as more and more people are), this book will help you prepare for your next role.

Applicants who were slam-dunked with retrenchment after being in the same job for yonks, this book will help you get back on track to get a new and better job.

Mature aged applicants with a dinosaur résumé from ten years ago (or no résumé), this book will teach you how to write a winning résumé and cover letter from scratch – we'll take you step-by-step through the process.

Applicants who don't know how 80% of recruiters and employers use key words and robot scanners. You need to read this book if you want to get a job in today's tough job market.

Applicants who don't have a professional LinkedIn Profile, you'll be behind the eight ball when it comes to recruiters and employers checking you out to offer you a job.

Graduates looking for your first job - read this book and then read *Get That Government Job* for everything you need to know about getting a private sector or government job.

Applicants interested in getting a government job but don't know beans about answering selection criteria (now called key capabilities), this book will shine a little light for you – then read *Get That Government Job* for the nitty-gritty stuff.

Acknowledgements

I am indebted to my clients who allowed me to use their "real" applications in this book (of course, I changed personal information to protect their privacy).

Each of these clients faced the same challenges of getting a job as you are now facing. After reading this book, they succeeded in writing scanner-friendly applications using key words...and so can you.

Thank you to my amazing family for your love and patience while I write. A huge thank you to my daughter, Tasha, for doing the formatting for this book.

Thank you also to Polly and Willie, my writing "companion dogs" who happily sit under my desk, day and night. I keep fit throwing squeaker toys and tennis balls between chapters.

Table of Contents

Introduction

Have you been sending off your résumé that worked really well a few years ago, but now isn't getting you to a single interview? It's very disheartening, but there's a good reason for this happening.

Your résumé that was previously successful in getting you to an interview won't cut the mustard now without 'key words' tailored to each individual job and scanner-friendly formatting.

The world of work has changed dramatically in the last decade with technology now being used to cull large numbers of applications for more and more limited roles.

Here's how it works. Applicant Tracking Systems (ATS) aka 'robot readers' are used by at least 80% of companies in Australia and more than 90% of companies in the U.S. to screen large numbers of job applications and then rank them on how well they match the requirements of the role. They do this by looking for 'key words' that the employer or recruiter has selected that match the requirements in the Position Description (PD) or job advertisement.

So, if your application doesn't contain sufficient key words, you will get a 'thumbs down' from the robot scanner and won't progress to the 'human reader' stage.

Also, you need to learn a new way of formatting your document to enable robot scanners to 'read' your application. You may have written a very pretty application using a template you downloaded from the internet. If it has fancy fonts, boxes, underlines and graphics, it's very likely the robots won't be able to read anything on your application.

You need to use the KISS Principle in formatting your document – Keep It Simple Sweetheart!

In this book, we will cover everything you need to know about THE NEW RULES of writing job applications to make your résumé work for both robot readers and human readers. You will also learn how to 'sell' yourself in your application and in your LinkedIn Profile to get you over the line.

If you're like most career changers, you've spotted a great job and you need your résumé makeover ... yesterday. No problem. We've made it really easy for you to update your résumé and cover letter quickly and painlessly with templates where you replace the sample text with your own information. Easy! Peasy!

We've also provided valuable QUICK GUIDES, CHEAT SHEETS and CHECKLISTS to make sure your application is free of errors that could end your career before it starts.

Grab a coffee and let's get started on your new career.

Chapter 1

Getting a handle on today's new job market

The structure of Australia's workforce has changed dramatically in the last few decades. At that time, around one in ten employees worked part-time – now, it's one in four who work part time.

Some workers prefer the flexibility of part time employment to achieve a work/life balance, while others would prefer to be in full time work. The term for those who want to work full time, but can't get full time jobs is 'underemployment'.

In January 2017, there were 11.9 million Australians employed, the largest number on record. Of these, 8.2 million were in full time employment with 3.7 million in part time employment.

Job trends – more contract and part time roles

Older job seekers will remember when you started in a job and stayed in that career for life. A teacher stayed a teacher until retirement. A bank manager started as a teller and worked through the ranks in the bank. Now, it's a different story with certainty of employment a thing of the past. There are fewer full time jobs – most are contract roles and part time positions which help employers ride out uncertain economic times.

Even government jobs that used to be the safest long term jobs around are now predominantly short term 'contract roles' where applicants apply for their own positions each year.

Summing up the current employment market

1. *The Australian Employment Outlook to November 2019 Report* states that those with a Bachelor degree or higher will have the best chance of success in employment .

2. Instead of being in one role for your whole career as it was two decades ago, you will have a dozen or more jobs during your working life, so adaptability is a skill you need to develop.

3. There are far fewer permanent jobs available now – most are part time or contract roles to enable organisations to react quickly to economic situations.

4. There's a large increase in temporary and part time jobs. Contractors and freelancers often choose part time employment but there are many others who would prefer a full time role, but can't get one. This situation is referred to as 'underemployment'.

5. Because of the increased demand for employment (especially full time employment) companies recruit selectively to fill limited jobs using scanning software to 'cull' the large numbers of applications for each advertised position.

6. Job seekers will need to learn the 'new rules' about writing their applications with keywords to get past scanners to get to an interview.

'New Rules' for successful career changers

To be competitive in this new environment, you need to plan for your next job while you are in the current one. It's not a case of 'if' you lose your job – it's more likely 'when' you lose your job. This is the new 'Normal'. Here are some valuable tips to get you ready for that next move:

* Maintain your professional development

* Keep up-to-the-minute with new technology

* Network with colleagues regularly

* Keep in touch with previous employers

* Get a professional LinkedIn profile

* Join employment groups on LinkedIn and participate in forums

* Develop new skill sets to enable you to move easily and quickly to new roles

The key to your success is your ability to reinvent yourself and your career - adapt quickly to new environments, learn new skills and think outside the square about career choices.

Chandler Macleod Recruitment sums up this new world of work:
'Whether you're new to the workforce, contemplating a career change, or returning after a break, researching industry and employment trends is a fantastic way to ensure you're making informed career decisions. Armed with this information, you can identify which sectors are expected to provide stability, get an understanding of how competitive a particular industry is likely to be, and determine whether or not you should upskill or pursue study before applying for jobs. Of course, while it is impossible to get any foolproof predictions around future industry performance, analysing job ad statistics and labour data can lead to some interesting revelations.'

Armed with with this information, you can identify which sectors are expected to provide stability, get an understanding of how competitive a particular industry is likely to be, and determine whether or not you should upskill or pursue study before applying for jobs.

Of course, while it is impossible to get any foolproof predictions around future industry performance, analysing job ad statistics and labour data can lead to some interesting revelations.'

Chapter 1: Summary

The Employment Outlook Report predicts that a Bachelor Degree or higher will increase your chance of success in the job market – so, if you're tossing up about doing further study, the answer is 'YES'.

There's a strong trend toward part time employment – from 1 in 10 two decades ago, to 1 in 4 now.

There are 'new rules' for successful career changers. This is particularly important for people in contract roles who need to prepare for their next job while still in the current one.

To be competitive in the new workplace environment, you need to maintain your professional development and keep up-to-the-minute with new technology, network with colleagues, keep in touch with previous employers, get a professional social media profile and develop new skill sets to enable you to move to new roles seamlessly.

Chapter 2

The story of Application Tracking Systems (ATS)

Twenty years ago, you applied for a job by answering a classified ad in the newspaper. You typed (you may have even hand-written) your applications and posted them using snail mail. With the rise in popularity of the internet, particularly in the last decade, the recruitment process moved quickly from paper-based applications to email and eventually to online job portals. 'Monster' was the leader of the pack in online recruitment. To help manage the large number of applications, hiring managers needed to develop an efficient electronic system.

Here's a brief timeline of how ATS came into being

1991: World Wide Web enables development of electronic Job Boards such as 'Monster'

1994: Job Boards become more popular – 'Monster', 'Netstart' and 'Career Builder'

1996: Martin Quelett, a Canadian, developed a French language Job Board called 'Viasite'

1999: Martin Quelett renamed his business 'Recruitsoft.inc.'

2003: LinkedIn was founded

2004: I wrote *Selection Criteria Toolkit* to help applicants understand the importance of key words needed for government job applications

2005: Hiring managers needed a system for managing large numbers of applications from very popular online job boards

2006: I wrote *'Get That Government Job'* to help applicants come to terms with key words needed to answer selection criteria for government jobs

2009: I wrote a second edition of *Get That Government Job* – key words were very much part of everyday recruitment by this time

2012: 'TALEO' (the largest ATS provider) acquired 'Recruitsoft', 'Recruitmax' and 'Vurv'

2013: 'TALEO' had 20 million users and LinkedIn had 225 million users

2017: There are hundreds of ATS providers and more than 80% of employers use them as an essential part of their recruitment process

Why are Applicant Tracking Systems Used?

An applicant tracking system (ATS) is a software application that enables the electronic handling of recruitment needs. There are applications to suit all sized businesses, even free and open source ATS software is available. Sometimes these systems are called 'robots' or 'robot scanners'.

Applicant tracking systems are used to help ease the workload of recruiters and hiring managers. The internet makes it fast and easy for job seekers to apply for jobs. In fact, job board sites like Monster, Indeed, SEEK, Careerone and other online job portals allow job seekers to apply for a job using a saved résumé with only one click.

Research on these sites show that for every corporate job posting, there are up to 250 applications. Of these candidates, only 4 – 6 will be contacted for an interview. Imagine the cost and workload of screening these applications manually.

In order to make the recruitment process more manageable, applicant tracking software has become entrenched in both large and small organisations. *The Wall Street Journal* reports that résumé screening software is used by more than 90% of larger companies in the United States. In Australia, the figure is about 80%, but is growing due to inexpensive systems suitable for smaller organisations.

Here's how Applicant Tracking Systems work

The recruiter might request the following: 'Top 20 candidates for the position of Marketing Manager according to the criteria entered.' The criteria will contain the key words related to the requirements of the job as listed in the Position Description (PD).

CLICK. The software spits out a list that contains the top 20 candidates and their rankings. It's much easier for the recruiter to manage 20 applicants rather than the original 200.

This is fantastic for the recruiter in time saving and efficiency, but how about the candidate who has spent hours writing their application that doesn't see the light of day?

Not so good!

The ATS cannot recognise certain formatting elements and many excellent candidates miss being selected for the next stage of the recruitment process - human readers. In marketing, we talk about KISS – Keep It Simple Sweetheart. This acronym works perfectly for the ATS. Eliminate fancy formatting elements and keep all text aligned to the left. Use true-type sans serif fonts (the ones that come with your computer) such as Arial, Verdana, Calibri, Tahoma, Trebuchet and Garamond. Go to the QUICK FORMATTING GUIDE for detailed explanations.

Robot readers and human readers

Applicant Tracking Systems are usually the first part of the recruitment screening process as they enable the recruiter or employer to process large numbers of applications efficiently and come up with a ranking of how well each applicant matches the requirements of the job.

Recruiters decide on the key words for each individual position and program the ATS to look for those key words. Applications that don't have the key words will not move on to the next stage of the recruitment process.

The trick for candidates is in identifying and finding the key words and phrases. The keywords and phrases are usually concrete, measurable skills required to perform the job competently. These are called 'hard skills'. They also look for 'soft skills'. For example, if you are applying for a job as a 'Course Trainer', a recruiter may search for hard skills such as 'Certificate IV in Training and Assessment' and 'course developer'. Recruiters may also look for 'soft skills' such as' communication skills'. We'll go into how to identify 'key words and phrases a little later'.

The downside of ATS is that excellent candidates are missed by résumé screening robots with 75% of applicants being rejected before their applications are read by a human decision maker.

This is because they haven't written their résumés to comply with the résumé screening software. Don't let that happen to you. Read the QUICK FORMATTING GUIDE to skip past the scanners.

So, what happens to applications in the next stage of the recruitment process?

The ATS provides a ranking based on how well the candidates meet the requirements of the role. These applications then progress to the 'yes' pile to be read by a human reader with a different set of criteria to impress.

You have only 6 seconds to convince the human reader that you have what it takes.

These readers will probably be people who understand the role such as HR specialists or managers in that section. They will be looking at how well you'll fit within their organisation. They'll also be looking at what you've achieved for former employers as a gauge of what you can do for them. Please go to Chapter 5: How to 'sell yourself' in your résumé with achievements for detailed explanations.

The last stage is proofreading your document to ensure it is error free. Just one spelling mistake could cost you the job. **Download the QUICK PROOFREADING GUIDE to catch any problems.**

Chapter 2: Summary

Great applicants are missed by résumé screening software with 75% of candidates being rejected before their applications are read by a human decision maker.

On average, 250 applications are received for a corporate role – only 4-6 applicants will get an interview.

You need to write and format your application to get past the digital scanners looking for key words and phrases in order to progress to a human reader.

Your résumé has to be formatted using a KISS approach to be able to be read by the scanners – no fancy formatting, boxes, underlining or graphics.

Writing a successful job application requires attention to detail, correct formatting and using key words from the PD.

Chapter 3

Looking for Key Words and Phrases

You are already familiar with key words and phrases through using search engines such as Google and Yahoo to find information for you. If you need a plumber and you live on the Gold Coast, you'd type in key words such as 'plumbers Gold Coast' and will come up with a choice of plumbers in those areas.

Similarly, the recruiter or employer programs in key words and phrases required to perform the job. These key words could include: the position title, qualifications, skills, years of experience in the industry, or even your postcode.

For example, for the role of 'Marketing Manager', the key words might include the following:

* Job title e.g. (Marketing Manager)

* Company Name (XYZ Company)

* Postcode (4218)

* Hard Skills (Marketing Campaigns; Copywriting)

* Soft Skills (Communication Skills)

* Technical terms, such as specific software (Indesign; Photoshop)

* Qualifications/ Educational Levels (Bachelor of Business) or (Certificate IV in Business)

* Industry buzzwords and acronyms (Customer Relationship Management) (CRM)

* Company/university names (University of Queensland) (UQ)

* Professional organisations (Australian Institute of Management) (AIM)

The scanner then looks for these key words and rates applications on how closely they match the requirements of the job. Only those with a high ranking will move through the selection process onto the next stage, which is a review by a human reader.

Following is a real example of a section of a Position Description and an excerpt from a winning application that scored the applicant an interview within 24 hours of clicking 'send'.

Example of key words in a Position Description (PD) for Regional Sales Manager role

Below is a job posting for a Regional Sales Manager and the key words. Most are 'hard skills' (skills that are concrete and measurable like 'sales' and 'sales management') but there are also a few 'soft skills' like self-motivated' and 'enthusiastic'.

If you don't include these keywords, your application won't get past the robots.

Regional Sales Manager

J2040 - Brisbane, QLD

- Brisbane, QLD

- Excellent Career Opportunity

Our client, an industry leader in the manufacture and marketing of brand name Agchemical products, is seeking to appoint an enthusiastic and motivated Regional Sales Manager

The successful candidate will be responsible for developing and implementing marketing strategies to optimise sales and profitability of the product portfolio. You will achieve sales and profitability goals within the defined territory through effective business planning and development with distribution customers and resellers.

Responsibilities include:

- Manage and support distribution channels to improve performance

- Negotiate and implement key reseller business and promotional plans

- Set and achieve sales budgets and seek out and secure new business

- Drive demand at key resellers, distributors and key influencers

- Provide technical assistance, training and presentations to customers, agronomists and end users

- Analyse and communicate market competitor and customer trends.

Commercially focused, you will be self-motivated, reliable, capable of working unsupervised with highly developed interpersonal and communication skills. The successful candidate will have a proven track record in sales management and achievement, complemented by exposure to broadacre and horticulture cropping systems. The ability to plan and manage your time and the confidence to negotiate at all levels of the distribution channel would be seen as essential.

A salary commensurate with the responsibilities of the role will be negotiated. A fully maintained company vehicle is provided.

Agribusiness Recruitment Pty Ltd thanks all applicants. However, only those to be interviewed will be contacted.

For confidential enquiries call Joe Bloggs on 00 000 000 and Email your resume to joebloggs@agrecruit.com.au quoting J2040 or apply via www.agrecruit.com.au

---

Fig. 3.0 Key Words on the Regional Sales Manager PD

Use the key words and the language of the job

Look for keywords and use the language of the job. To find these keywords, go to SEEK or some other job portal and look up the role you are interested in. Then note the requirements for that role. For example, if you are applying for an IT Systems and Network Manager job, you'd look for words such as: network design; systems management; LAN administration; project planning and management; product and design research; vendor interface and negotiation; systems conversion; systems implementation, disaster recovery; system migrations, applications support, etc.

Similarly, if you were looking for key words for an *Operations and Logistic Manager* role, you'd look for key words such as: Operations Systems; strategic planning; cost management; facilities design; offshore production; inventory management; manufacturing process; quality control; OH&S; EEO; anti-discrimination; compliance; supplier partnership; etc.

Keyword Density: Repeat important key words as often as they are mentioned in the PD

For example, if the key word 'OH&S' is used 3 times in the PD, find 3 places to use this term in your résumé. You could easily do this by using it once in your Professional Profile and then in the Skills section, followed by another mention in your Achievements.

Key words and Acronyms

When used in résumés, acronyms can be confusing for both the robot reader and the human reader. Furthermore, an acronym in one industry might mean something else in another industry. To eliminate this problem, the first time you use a term write it in full, followed by the acronym in brackets e.g. Customer Relationship Management (CRM).

How to find frequently used résumé keywords for certain industries

Sites such as the three listed below keep track of keyword-related statistics.

Indeed.com/Job Trends
https://www.indeed.com/jobtrends

This site contains graphs showing how many job advertisements contain particular search terms, gathered from many thousands of postings on employment sites.

The New York Department of Labour
https://www.labor.ny.gov/agencyinfo/industrykeywords.shtm

This site contains a list of suggested résumé keywords for candidates seeking jobs in a variety of industries:

Australian Government Job Outlook
http://www.joboutlook.gov.au/

Job Outlook is a careers and labour market research information site covering around 350 individual occupations.

Common Industry Key Words

Following are common key words from 5 key industries:

Management
Continuous Process Improvement; Account Management; Cost Reduction; Team Leadership; Strategic Plan; Strategic Development; Corporate communications: Executive Management; Executive Presentation; Corporate Culture.

Accounting/Finance
Accounts Management; Partnership Accounting; Risk Management; Due Diligence; Equity; Feasibility Analysis; Investor Relations; Strategic Planning; Compliance; Corporate Tax; Accounts Receivable; Asset Management

Sales and Marketing
Sales Team; Account Management; Client Relationship Management (CRM); Product Lifecycle; Business Development; Sales Team Building; Sales Training; Market Surveys; Market Research; Sales Presentations; Sales Forecasting; Sales Targets; Sales Budgets; Product Launch; Research and Development (R & D).

Human Resources
Applicant Screening; Applicant Tracking' Employee Development; Employee Training; Training and Development; Employee Performance; Incentive Planning; Position Classification; Compensation; Competency.

Technical/Engineering
Feasibility Analysis; ROI; R & D; Specifications; Statistical Analysis; Regulatory Compliance; Resource Management; Product Design; Product Development Cycle; Product Reliability; Project Planning; OH&S; Project Management.

How to generate Key Words using a Word Cloud

There's another way to help you find key words using 'word cloud' technology. You may have seen word clouds in social media displaying metadata on Wordpress blogs. *Wordle* and *TagCrowd* offer the opportunity to paste a document such as the PD into the generator box and set options for your word cloud. It's a good indicator, but don't rely on this method alone.

TagCrowd works by counting the frequency of every word in your source text and visualizing the top N of these as a word cloud. You set the value of N with this field. The appropriate value will depend on your application and the size of your source text. In general, it's better to use smaller clouds for shorter source texts and larger clouds for longer source texts.

You can choose to display the actual number of times each word appears in your text source. This is helpful so that you can use a similar 'word density' in your application. For example, if the word 'sales' is mentioned three times, try to work it into your application at least that many times. You can do this in your Professional Summary, Skills and in your employment history. Also, you can mention it in your cover letter.

A word of caution - this software uses the standard Porter Stemming Algorithm to detect and combine similar words. For example, the words 'sales', 'selling' and 'sell' will all be combined so your word cloud is less redundant. This isn't necessarily a good thing for ATS, so make sure you use the actual form of the word provided in the PD in your application.

Fig. 3.1 Word Cloud of Regional Sales Manager PD

Word Clouds leave a bit to be desired in looking for key words. There are several applications that allow you to scan your résumé against the PD to see how it rates. One of the most popular is Jobscan which allows you to test your application and get a report on your overall ranking against the PD. It also advises which keywords are missing so you can rewrite your résumé and rescan to get a higher ranking. You need to get 80% or more to move to the 'yes' pile for human readers.

Try it for yourself:

Go the Jobscan Home Page (https://www.jobscan.co/#) where you'll find two boxes as below:

Step 1: Cut and paste your résumé and cover letter into the box on the left.

Then cut and paste the PD into the box on the right. Click 'Scan' and in a few seconds, you'll receive a report that shows key words, their frequency and how well you scored against the criteria. It's optimal to score 80% or higher to increase your chances of getting an interview.

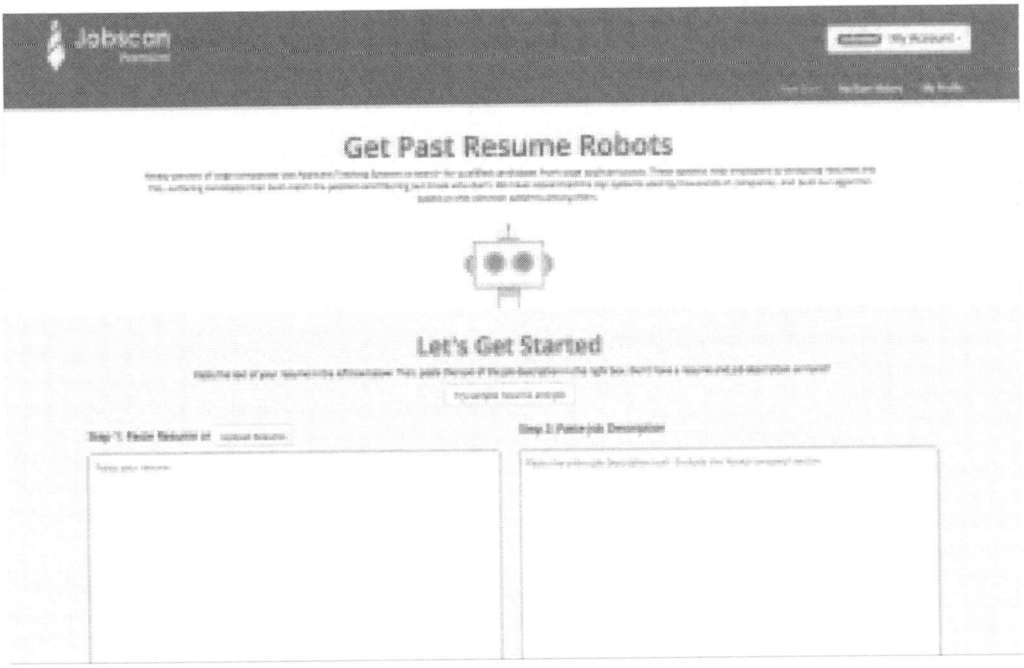

Fig. 3.2 Jobscan: scan your résumé against the PD Step

Step 2: Examine the Match Report for Skills and Keywords

Look at the keyword and skills Match Report underneath the overall résumé match rate. Be sure to note which keywords you've successfully included and which ones are missing. The more frequently a skill or keyword appears, the more important it is–and the more weight the ATS will place upon it.

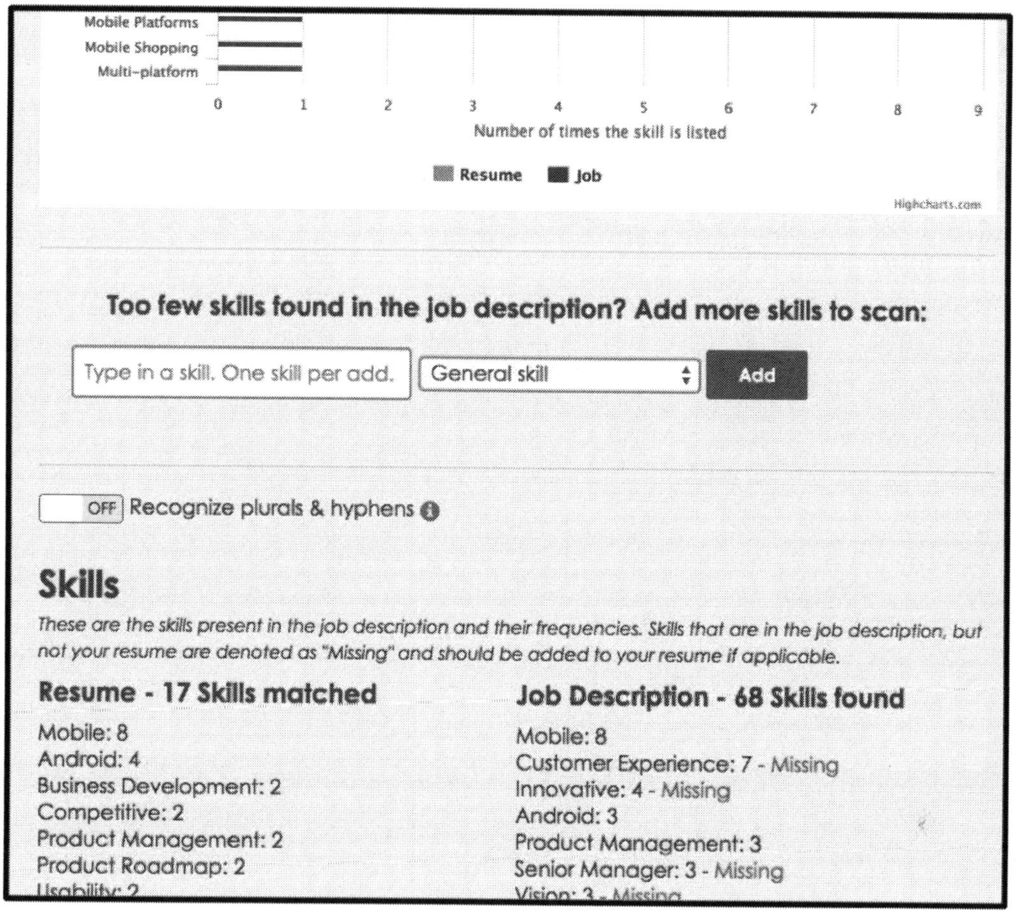

Fig. 3.3 Jobscan: Report

Step 3: Review Optimisation Suggestions

In addition to providing you with an instant résumé match rate, the Match Report also offers specific résumé optimisation tips. Once you've reviewed the entire Match Report, start incorporating each type of suggestion: skills, keywords, and optimisation. Use the exact wording from the job description in your résumé. Re-Scan against the job description until you reach an 80% success rate.

We told you it would be easy...and it is. Key words are the key to your job success.

Chapter 3: Summary

Key words and phrases can include: the position title, qualifications, skills, years' experience in the industry, nouns and noun phrases ...even your postcode.

The employer programs in key words and phrases required to perform the requirements of the job. If you don't have these key words in your application, you will not progress to the 'yes' pile.

Use the language of the job, including common acronyms.

Use the same density of key words as the PD. For example, if the PD mentions 'customer service' four times, try to use the key words a similar number of times.

Chapter 4

How to format your résumé to keep the robots happy and go to the 'yes' pile for human readers

Keep in mind the KISS Principle – Keep It Simple Sweetheart – no fancy bullets, text boxes, tables, photos, underlining or unusual headings. Robots get confused with fancy formatting and will 'bin' your application long before a human reader sees it.

12 Point Formatting Guide:

1. Headers and Footers

Avoid using headers and footers in your résumé because they may jam the algorithms on some ATS software. It's safer to keep contact information in the body of the document to ensure it doesn't get lost.

2. You will need a custom résumé for every job

Use actual wording from the job description in your résumé. For example, if a nursing job PD asks for someone with 'triage experience' or 'primary care experience', be sure that your résumé contains 'triage experience' or 'primary care experience'.

3. Don't include a photo in your résumé

Don't include a photo in your résumé unless it's a requirement of the role, such as for acting or modelling. However, do include a professional photo in your LinkedIn profile to build trust. Most recruiters and employers check out LinkedIn profiles as part of the recruitment and selection process.

4. Text Boxes and Tables

Text boxes and tables are common formatting elements that give your document a professional look. ATS are getting more and more sophisticated in what they can recognise but it's safer to use plain formatting. If the ATS can't recognise the field, it will show up blank. Imagine what happens to a résumé written completely within a text box. Disaster! Some of the templates available for purchase online are written this way. Don't use them. Use hard set tabs to format your document.

5. Use the reverse chronological format – avoid the functional format

The ATS is developed to parse chronological résumés – not functional résumés that are designed to disguise gaps in employment. Make sure you account for periods of time when you are out of the workforce to avoid being given a poor ranking by the robots. Nine out of ten recruiters prefer the reverse chronological format because it is easier to read.

6. Typography and Layout

Sans serif fonts like Courier, Arial, Verdana and Helvetica work best on screens, while serif fonts like Times New Roman are easier to read in printed documents. Keep your formatting simple by using a universal font (the ones that come with your computer) that will look the same on the recruiter's screen as they do on yours. The best point sizes to use are 14 point for headers and 10-12 point for body text.

7. Name your file professionally

Put your name and the position you are applying for in the file name or it may get lost. Call your résumé 'Mary Smith_ Finance Manager.' Don't call your document just 'Mary Smith_Résumé'.

8. Use common headings in your résumé

Use common headings the robots will look for such as: Professional Profile, Skills, Career Highlights, Professional Experience, Employment Experience, Employment History, Qualifications, Education and Training so that the robots will recognise your headings. Don't use uncommon headings such as Further Information, Added Value, Unpaid Employment, Personal Referees, Unpaid Work Experience, Hobbies, etc.

9. Use white space to break up your document and make it easy to read

White space is one of the most important layout elements. Don't make the common mistake of using a small font size and trying to squeeze everything onto the page to make your résumé shorter. If your résumé is hard to read, the human reader will simply go 'next'.

10. Present the information in your Employment Experience in the same order

Use the sequence of: company name, location, position title and dates of employment, starting with the most recent job. Consistency in formatting looks professional and makes the document easier to read.

11. Be thorough with proofreading

Incorrect spelling and grammar will quickly get your application binned. Don't rely solely on your computer's spellchecker. It won't pick up where you use an incorrect homonym (words that sound the same but have a different meaning) such as 'there' instead of 'their'.

12. Use bold and italics (but not underline) to make your document look professional

Avoid underlining words because this can affect the legibility of lower case descenders (the parts of the letter below the line) of letters such a, g, j and y. The scanners get confused with underlined words.

Chapter 4: Summary

Avoid fancy formatting and use the KISS principle to ensure your application is read by the scanners and goes in the 'yes' pile for human readers.

You will need a custom résumé for every job you apply for -use the actual key words from the PD in your résumé.

Use common headings in your résumé to make sure the scanners can recognise what you've written. If you use unfamiliar headings, the page will be blank.

Use the PROOFREADING QUICK GUIDE to make sure your application is free from errors. It only takes one or two errors to have your application binned.

You can kickstart your application using the formatted templates that come with this book. Simply replace the text with your own information to get a résumé that is ATS friendly.

Chapter 5

How to structure your résumé and tailor it for each role

We've already talked about the formatting problems that occur with some résumé templates available on the internet because they aren't compliant with digital tracking systems. The templates that come with this book are ATS-Friendly and have been tested on several ATS scanners. They also have 'common' headers that robots recognise. The key to success is to use the KISS Formula – 'Keep It Simple Sweetheart'. Follow this quick guide for writing a résumé that both robot and human readers will love. Print out the Résumé Headings Summary for easy reference when you start writing your résumé. The list is in the Resources for Career Changers at the end of the book.

Work out the headings you will use in your résumé

Make sure you use the first page of your résumé to 'sell' your most important assets. If you have an extensive work history, you might use the first five headings on this list in this order. For graduates, you might replace 'Career Highlights' with your Qualifications. Here's a quick explanation for each heading to get your started. More info follows:

Example for a Graduate:
Professional Profile
Educations/ Qualifications
Professional Skills
Employment Experience (this might include part time employment or practical placements at university)

Example for someone with less than five years' experience:
Professional Profile
Professional Skills
Selected Achievements
Employment Experience
Qualifications
Professional Memberships

Example for someone at an advanced level:
Professional Skills
Career Highlights
Professional Experience
Professional Memberships
Board Roles

Résumé Headings	Tips for their use
Position Title/Contact Details	This is placed at the top of your résumé and includes your Name, Suburb, City, Job Title, Position Number, Email Address and Mobile.
Professional Profile	A few sentences that describe how you meet the requirements of the role and what you can do for the employer. This replaces the 'Career Objective' which focussed on what the employer could do for you.
Skills / Professional Skills	These are key words aligned to the PD. Hard skills include skills that can be measured, such as the position title, qualifications, and years of experience in the industry. Soft skills include phrases such as 'communication skills'.
Career Highlights/ Selected Achievements	Choose about six achievements that 'sell' your ability to do the job based on your previous experience. Use facts and figures to make this section credible.
Employment History/ Employment Experience/ Professional Experience/ Employment	This is where you list your employment starting form the most recent. Use a consistent format of Name of the Company, Location, Your Position and Dates of Employment. Underneath the main heading of the company name, write a short description of the company's core business. Always include 'Achievements under individual roles where you have excelled.
Professional Memberships/Board Roles	For senior roles, it is advantageous to include Board roles and Industry Memberships
Training/Professional Development	List relevant training courses, conferences and seminars. The purpose is to show the employer you are 'current' with your knowledge in your particular industry.
Technical Summary/ Project Management Summary	For those with IT or Project Management backgrounds, this is a helpful way to list your skills. Use it on your front page instead of 'Skills'. Include details of the project, including scope, budget, specifications and outcomes.
Education/ Qualifications	For graduates, this goes on the front page. For applicants with proven work histories, it is placed further back. For people with extensive histories, it may not be necessary to present it.
Referees	Choose three referees who can vouch for your performance in the workplace. Provide their relationship to you, email addresses and mobiles for easy contact. Cherish your referees and keep them informed about what you are doing in your career.

Fig. 5.0 Résumé Headings

'What to put where' in your updated résumé

You have only 6 seconds to grab the reader's attention. Make it work! Use the front page to list the most important information for 'selling you and your skills. For most applicants, you will use this space to showcase your experience, career highlights and professional skills. For graduates, you will use this space to 'sell' your professional qualifications.

1. Name, Position and Contact Details and Job Title (Front Page)

If you want a recruiter to contact you for an interview, make it easy for them to find your contact details. Name, position, address (suburb/city /state / postcode), email and phone number. Postcode is important for when the recruiter is looking to fill a role down the track and is looking for local staff. They will use the postcode as a key word.

Never use a hotmail address. It looks very unprofessional. Instead, get a free gmail address. Use your first and last name combination if it's available, otherwise ad your middle initial or a number. e.g. FredGBrowning@gmail.com or Fred.Browning3355@gmail.com

Example of a strong Job Title:

Here's a strong title for your résumé that's clear and professional. It's better to put this information in the body of the document, rather than the header section.

John Smith

Broadbeach, Gold Coast 4218   Phone: 0000 000 000   Email: jsmith@somedomain.com

Marketing and Communications Manager

Fig 5.1. Name, Position and Contact Details and Job Title (Front Page)

2. Replace the Career Objective from old résumés with a Professional Profile

One of the first things that 'dates' your résumé is the presence of a Career Objective. It's 'old hat' and may also imply to the reader that you are stuck in the past. A career objective tells an employer what you want, while a Professional Profile tells an employer what you can do for them. A Professional Profile is usually two or three sentences and is the written equivalent of an 'elevator pitch' – it's what you would say to a potential employer to 'sell your skills and yourself' in 20 seconds or less. Here's an example of a Professional Profile for a Marketing Communications Manager:

- National award-winning marketing professional with 15 years of experience leading corporate marketing and internal communications for high net worth companies across diverse industries.
- Proficient in leading creative teams, multimedia divisions and corporate communications departments in the creation of marketing campaigns that achieved corporate objectives and built corporate brands.

Fig. 5.2 Professional Profile (Front Page)

The aim of the profile is to demonstrate who you are and what you can do for an employer.

3. Career Highlights

Link these statements to the requirements of the PD using key words and phrases. This can be a few bullet points or a few sentences that show how you have the skills, experience and achievements that match the requirements of the job. Use the Situation, Action, Outcome (SAO) technique to write a short paragraph.

Example 1:

(S) 'In my role as Marketing Manager at XYZ,

(A) I managed excessive customer complaints through developing and implementing training for staff in customer service.

(O) The result was a 25% reduction in customer complaints in just 2 months, and a 27% increase in sales over the next 12 months reporting period.

Example 2:

(S) As the Team Leader for the Basic Environmental Assessment for a gold refinery's nickel and copper plant expansion project,

(A) I compiled a Water Use License application for a large ferromanganese producer, including a water balance for the plant site, a review of existing licenses as well as compilation of new licensing reports and documents.

(O) I developed the Environmental Management Plan (EMP) for this producer, including site visits to assess current production practices. I identified potential and ongoing environmental impacts as well as a desktop review of process balances and material flows, culminating in training plant personnel against the contents of the EMP.

Figure 5.3 shows how this section looks in your resume:

CAREER HIGHLIGHTS

- Proficient in cost-effective marketing management and vendor negotiations resulting in exceeding business growth objectives by approximately 20% per annum in line with the strategic plan.

- Developed and launched integrated, multi-channel print, catalogue, web and direct marketing campaigns that increased sales from $2.9M (2007) to $9.7M by 2010 year end.

- Initiated and directed market launch of 21 new products. Identified opportunities, conducted feasibility studies on new products, collaborated with engineering team and created campaigns generating in excess of $2.6M in annual sales.

- Expanded B2B client base by 69% in three years by consistently delivering goal-surpassing marketing results and ensuring complete client satisfaction.

- Regular winner of numerous awards for excellence in marketing: Award of Excellence for Outstanding Advertising *(ABC Co 'XYZ Campaign' campaign)*, 2014; Gold Award for Outstanding Advertising *(ABC Co "XYZ" direct mail campaign)*, 2012; 2008; Action Award for Outstanding Advertising *(ABC Co "XYZ" campaign)*, 2007.

Fig. 5.3 Career Highlights (First or Second Page)

4. Key Skills /Professional Skills

Focus on 'hard skills' such as job titles, technical skills, industry experience, number of years in a particular role, and other key skills listed in the PD. Include up to 12 hard skills. If you see soft skills like communication skills, team skills, leadership skills, etc, coming up in the PD, you can attach these after the hard skills. Soft skills are sometimes included in the key words and phrases. Use tabs for the Skills columns (two or three columns) – not text boxes. This keyword section is very important for two reasons. It ensures you get past the robots with density of keywords early in your résumé and it also ensures the human reader can see at a glance how your skills match the job requirements. If you're fluent in another language and it's relevant to the role, list it as a skill.

Example from the Marketing Communication Manager role:

PROFESSIONAL SKILLS

- Development of Marketing Campaigns for diverse industries
- Liaison with corporate clients
- Leadership of creative teams
- Product Positioning & Branding

- Market Research/Data Analysis
- Compilation of Training Materials
- Social Media Campaigns
- Public & Media Relations
- New Product Launches

Fig. 5.4. Professional Skills (Front Page)

5. Employment History /Achievements

Use the format of company/position/dates to please the majority of ATS scanners. Give a short summary of the organisation's core business to set the context for the reader.

Here's an example for the Marketing Communication Manager role:

EMPLOYMENT

ABC COMPANY, Example City   **Aug. 2007 to Present:**
Multimillion dollar company selling automotive supplies and parts

Marketing Communications Manager,
Manage corporate marketing and communications functions, overseeing a $2.5M budget and 9 member team. Direct brand management, PR, media relations, corporate positioning, product launches, advertising, sales collateral and tradeshow marketing.

Selected Accomplishments:

- Led market launch of 27 new products. Identified opportunities, researched new product possibilities, collaborated with engineering team and created campaigns generating $2.9M in annual sales.

- Created web portal to transform previously archaic intranet into a dynamic website improving communication flow and adding an effective sales tool for sales representatives.

- Wrote catalogues, course guides and training brochures that enhanced the sales representatives' understanding of complex product features and helped them sell more effectively.

- Produced media kit that demonstrated key marketing analytics and demographics for use in sales presentations. Efforts were credited as instrumental in closing numerous high-level deals.

Fig. 5.5 Employment (Second Page)

For applicants with a short work history, it's okay to list a few key responsibilities of your jobs. However, make sure you highlight your achievements in each role. This is what 'sells' you to the employer. For applicants with extensive work histories, it's better to list only a few key responsibilities, as above, and focus on your achievements in each role.

If you work in a project management or IT role, you can list your key projects with a summary and achievements under each project, including scope, budget, specifications and outcomes.

You can also use the employment section for volunteer work, internships and unpaid positions.

Employers will always look for people who have been successful in former roles. This is because your past achievements are a good indicator of your future achievements. **Please see the next section for further information about 'selling' your achievements.**

You may have 20 years' experience... or more in the workplace – DO NOT list every job you've ever had. Only list the roles you've had in the last 10 years. You can do a section after this called 'Former Key Roles' and list one line for each position that is relevant to this role.

6. Qualifications / Education

Include the full name of the qualification and its acronym, as well as where you attained this qualification. Recruiters want to see if an applicant is qualified for the advertised position.

7. Training or Professional Development

This shows that you are dedicated to keeping your skills up to date, but it doesn't deserve first page status. It's often placed after the Employment Section. You can include any awards or courses that are relevant to the role you are applying for.

8. Professional Memberships or Board Roles

For senior roles, it's beneficial to include Professional Memberships or Board Roles. These may even be included in the key words for the role.

9. Referees

Usually, it's better not to include referees unless you are asked to do so or if you are writing an application for a government job. However, some recruiters, like Hays Recruitment, prefer to have two referees listed with your application. Follow the instructions on the PD.

When choosing referees, look for managers or colleagues who have worked directly with you and who can comment on your work performance. Keep them up to date with your applications so that when they are contacted, they will respond positively, rather than have to think where they knew you.

Your referees are your silent sales team – what they say about you can get you the job...or lose you the job. So, treat them with the greatest respect and thank them.

10. Residency Status

This is sometimes a requirement. Place this on the last page if it is a requirement for the role and also mention it in your cover letter.

11. LinkedIn/ Social Media

LinkedIn provides an opportunity to show a different side of you to a recruiter. Make sure your profile reflects the image you want to create. You can include relevant presentations, videos and photos that build and expand your image. Make sure your photo is professional. Please see section on 'Building your Brand' on Linkedin.

How to 'sell yourself' in your résumé with achievements

A lot of people have trouble working out the difference between a responsibility and an achievement.

If you're employed as a staff trainer, then 'writing training materials' is a responsibility. If you achieved outstanding results from your training that increased profitability by 23% in 9 weeks and reduced customer complaints by 55%, that's an achievement....and it's measurable!

To work out your achievements, think about the difference between when you started in a particular role and the situation when you left the role. What changes did you make? How did you do it? What did you achieve?

The Marketing Law of Specificity states that people remember facts and figures, rather than general statements. Think of some of the famous adverts of our times: Nescafe Coffee – 43 beans in every cup; Heinz Soup – 57 different varieties of soup. Another strange thing about marketing, people remember odd numbers more than even ones.

When listing your achievements, think in terms of measurable increases, decreases, cost savings and increased efficiencies for the organisation – not for yourself. Facts and figures (especially odd numbers) build your credibility. Be specific.

Here are some questions to ask yourself to identify your achievements:

1. Did you increase sales in the organisation? Use real figures or express it as a percentage and state the period of time.

Example: Increased sales by 23% in the first month through training frontline staff in customer service and developing staff incentives for excellence.

2. Did you grow the business through generating new business or bringing in new clients?

Example: Expanded B2B client base by 57% in three years through conducting monthly informational seminars for clients.

3. Did you save the organisation money or time? If so, how much and how did it work? Did you *develop* a new system or process? If so, what were the results?

Example: Saved XYZ organisation $725,000 per annum through implementing new guidelines to reduce workplace injury. These strategies have been adopted nationally.

4. Did you introduce any new or more effective systems for increasing productivity? If so, is your approach being used?

Example: Created web portal to transform previously archaic intranet system into a dynamic website that enables sales representatives to promote their products more efficiently. It has resulted in 33% increase in national sales in the past 12 months.

Chapter 5: Summary

Tailoring Tips:
Change the job title (include reference numbers if provided) for each individual job you apply for.

Change your Professional Profile section for each role using key words from each individual PD.

Adapt your career highlights to align with the PD, using key words.

Adapt your achievements to align with the PD, using key words.

If you supply referees, make sure they are able to comment on your background in relation to this role.
Change your LinkedIn profile in line with the PD using key words.

Write a list of your achievements and keep handy near the computer for when you are writing job applications. You can then tailor these achievements to fit in with the key words in each PD.

Chapter 6

10 Easy Steps to writing your job application

This example is for a School Administration Officer Position, but you can substitute your own information as you work through the steps.

STEP #1: Download the PD, job advertisement and other relevant documents

Analyse the Job Description, website, job advertisement and other material you can find online to identify the organisation's core messages and key words. Use these key words and phrases wherever applicable – especially in your Professional Summary, Skills and Achievements.

Applicant Information Package (Non –Teaching Vacancies)

Thank you for your interest in working with the **Department of Education and Training (DET)**. This Applicant Information Package is provided to assist applicants understand the departmental recruitment and selection process for Non-Teaching vacancies. You are encouraged to read this information carefully prior to applying.

WORKING FOR DET

*Inspiring Minds.
Creating opportunities
Shaping Queensland's future.*

DET is committed to ensuring Queenslanders have the education and skills they need to contribute to the economic and social development of Queensland.

DET touches the lives of over 1 million Queenslanders every day and has a presence, whether physical or virtual, in every community across the state.

Our customers range from:

- children, families, carers and non-government organisations
- students, families, carers and communities in school education
- students, apprentices and trainees, employers and industry in training and employment.

More information about DET, our strategic plan, key initiatives and organisational structure is available on our website – www.deta.qld.gov.au

Great People

DET is the largest employer in the state. It is our people that make the difference to the lives of Queenslanders

DET employees are required to actively participate in consultation and communication with supervisors and management regarding health, safety and wellbeing issues and comply with all provisions of the relevant workplace health and safety legislation and related health, safety and wellbeing responsibilities and procedures developed by the department.

Emergency management and fire safety training is provided in the local context of the workplace. School based employees will also complete student protection related training.

Smoking policy

A non-smoking policy applies in Queensland government buildings, offices and motor vehicles.

Superannuation

QSuper is the superannuation fund for current (and former) Queensland Government workers and their spouses. For further information please visit the QSuper website: http://www.qsuper.qld.gov.au/

Information Management

Staff responsible for creating, collecting, maintaining, using, disclosing, duplicating and disposing of information, as well as managing and using communication devices (for example email, internet and telephone) and public resources (for example computers and network resources) must undertake these tasks in accordance with the DET's information management policies and procedures (for example recordkeeping, privacy, security and email usage).

Code of conduct

All departmental employees are required to uphold the Code of Conduct for the Queensland Public Service and the department's Standard of Practice. In addition, each employee is required to commit to the

Fig 6.0 Information Package

Role Description

Administrative Officer	Job Ad Reference	SER227602/16		
(Generic)	Job Evaluation No.	14038	TRIM No.	09/128349
	Work Unit	Palm Beach-Currumbin State High School State Schools Division		
	Location	South East Region		
	Classification	AO2 QLD Public Service Award – State 2012 36 ¼ hour week		
	Job Type	Temporary Part-Time 0.69 FTE until 8 December 2017 unless otherwise determined		
	Salary Range	$31 254 - $36 932 per annum *Plus superannuation contributions of up to 12.75% of your annual salary.*		
	Contact Officer	Robyn Rickard		
	Contact Telephone	07 5525 9333		
	Closing Date	Monday, 5 December 2016		

Your employer

The Department of Education and Training (DET) is committed to ensuring Queenslanders have the education and skills they need to contribute to the economic and social development of Queensland. The department delivers world class education and training services for people at every stage of their personal and professional development. We are also committed to ensuring our education and training systems are aligned to the state's employment, skills and economic priorities. DET is a diverse organisation with the largest workforce in the state. We provide services through four service delivery areas:

- State Schools Division delivers high quality education to more than 70 percent of all Queensland school students at prep, primary and secondary levels.

- Training and Skills Division works to meet the current and future needs of the economy through building a world class training and skilling system to enhance the skills of Queenslanders and optimise employment opportunities through the regulation of the state's apprenticeship and traineeship system, strategic investment in training and skills, and the provision of whole of government leadership on employment and labour market issues.

- Policy, Performance and Planning Division takes a strategic approach to driving the business of the portfolio, across, schooling, training and employment, early childhood, education and care and Indigenous education policy. The division engages in, policy development and intergovernmental relations, legislation, governance and planning, and monitors and reviews the department's performance framework.

Fig. 6.1 Position Description (Role Description)

The Position Description contains all of the information you need to write your application. It has the Duties and Responsibilities (Your Role) and, because this is a government job, it has selection criteria (now called Key Capabilities). If you are scratching your head trying to work out how on earth you could possibly reply to all of these points, you're not alone.

For private sector jobs, you usually only need a résumé and a cover letter which you attach to an online form.

We'll briefly cover how to apply for a government job in our Résumé Makeover for a school Administrative Officer role...just in case you decide this might be a good option for you later on.

Step #2: Get out your highlighter to mark key words and phrases and your examples

Analyse the Job Description, website, job advertisement and other material you can find online to identify the organisation's core messages and key words. Highlight every key word or phrase that you think is important. Make notes about your experience in relation to the PD (See Fig 6.2 below) and use these key words and phrases wherever applicable – especially in your Professional Summary, Skills and Achievements.

For example, under the sub heading of "General" in the PD below, it states: *Administer first aid to students (only in cases where the administrative officer agrees to be the school's nominated First Aid Officer".*

If you have a current First Aid Certificate, or are willing to acquire one, and agree to be the nominated First Aid Officer for the school, you will have an advantage over other applicants.

Key words are important for both applying for a particular role and also for when a recruiter or employer stores your resume on file for future roles.

When a position becomes available, they search their own databases to retrieve resumes using key words which include nouns, phrases, industry jargon and acronyms. For example, if the recruiter is filling a role as a Personal Assistant, they will look for keywords such as: Personal Assistant, PA, attention to details, organisational skills, diary management, meetings, confidentiality, records management and other related to that particular role. So, you need to have these key words in your resume and cover letter to get short-listed for an interview.

If you were applying for a position in customer service, some of the keywords that come to mind are: cash handling, reconciliation, customer, customer service, customer relationship, sales, add-on sales, retail, customer loyalty, etc.

Job ads provide lots of keywords where you can look up roles you are interested in and note the keywords used most often. Also, you can access a feature on LinkedIn that allows you to find the most commonly used terms for a particular role in a particular industry.

In Fig. 6.2 we have highlighted the keywords for the Administrative Officer role.

Excerpt from Position Description Administrative Officer

Your opportunity

As the Administrative Officer you will:

Contribute to the effective and efficient management and administration of the school by providing a high level of administrative support to the Principal/Business Services Manager.

- Develop and maintain the school's financial/administrative systems and procedures to ensure their efficiency and effectiveness.

Use these key words in Professional Summary and Skills Section

Use as an achievement to back up financial skills:
Accounts payable/receivable (9 years) including reducing debtors for ABC Resort from over 200k upon undertaking role to zero when I left.

Your role

You will have responsibility for leading the following activities and delivery of the following key tasks:

The duties performed by an administrative officer include a mix of any of the following activities.

General

- Recording and conveying important messages for staff and students.
- Administer first aid to students (only in cases where the administrative officer agrees to be the school's nominated first aid officer. In such cases the administrative officer would be required to be formally trained in the administration of first aid, and keep such qualifications current. All costs associated with obtaining and maintaining qualifications would be met from school funds).

Current First Aid Certificate- use in Professional Skills section and Cover Letter. Also add 'Blue Card for Working with Children' qualification and 'Cert 111 in Education Support' In Qualifications section

- Processing of incoming and outgoing mail, as well as delivering and collecting mail, parcels, documents etc.
- Perform a variety of other administrative or support services as directed.

25 years' experience in administrative support – use in Professional Summary, Cover Letter and Selection Criteria Statement (SCS)

Keyboard Skills

- Typing, including the undermentioned items: correspondence, minutes of meetings, policy documents, reports, forms, newsletters, prospectuses, memorandums, examination papers, class notes and School Annual Reports (AOP).
- Application of word processing and spreadsheet software systems knowledge and skills.

Computing Skills - proficient in word processing and spreadsheet software – Word, Excel, MYOB and numerous other software programs
Use in Professional Skills, Cover Letter and SCS

Keyboard Skills – typing of correspondence and reports 75 wpm 100% accuracy
Use in Professional Skills and Cover Letter

Fig. 6.2 Highlighted key words on PD

Keep this list near your computer so that you can refer to it when writing your résumé, cover letter and LinkedIn profile so that you cover all of the bases. Please note: The position title is always a key word, as is the Job Reference Number when provided.

Step #3: Read the PD instructions carefully

Check all links in the PD to gain insight into the ethos of the organisation, mission statement, etc. Make sure you follow all instructions, especially regarding how to lodge your application. Did you see the typo in this role description? Someone didn't proofread it correctly – don't let that happen to you.

Step #4: Open the résumé template

Save the document to your computer and change the name of the document.

Choose the headers you are going to use from the summary in the previous chapter. You can print out the page to keep as a ready reference near your computer.

Print out your highlighted PD with key words and your examples highlighted. Keep this near your computer as a ready reference also.

Replace the text in the résumé template with your own information. Use the language on the PD where possible to ensure the robots recognise the key words.

Use the key words in your Position Title, Profile, Skills Section and Employment History. It's very easy to use the main key words in these areas without 'stuffing' your résumé. Some applicants have tried to fool the robots by writing their key words over and over in white text. Don't do it. Your application will go to the bin.

Work through the résumé, following the above steps. It's a bit like following a recipe for chocolate cake – without the calories.

Step #5: Proofread your résumé

Check that you have followed the instructions provided on the PD.
Use the 'Proofreading Guide' to look for common errors.

Step #6: Check your résumé against the PD using Jobscan or similar provider

Download **www.jobscan.com** or other ATS that provides a similar service. and paste in your résumé and PD. Make any changes suggested and re-test until you achieve 80%. This will increase your chance of success in getting to an interview.

Step #7: Write your Cover Letter

Always write your résumé before you write your cover letter. Use the 'Cover Letter Guide' that follows, ensuring you use the key words and phrases you have identified and used in your résumé. If supplying a cover letter is optional, include it because it's another chance to sell your skills and experience.

Step #8: Update your LinkedIn Profile

Recruiters and employers regularly use LinkedIn and other social media as part of their selection process. You have a great opportunity to show your personality and achievements through the use of photos, videos and articles. Please read the 'LinkedIn Profile Guide'.

Step #9: Finalise and send off your application

Send your application, ensuring you follow the instructions on the PD. If possible, try to download the form before you start typing in those little boxes, so that you can see the 'big picture' first.

Step #10: Keep a copy of each application for easy reference when you get an interview or for your next application

Ensure you keep a copy all of the documents you downloaded and file away your application for future reference. You will need to access these notes and documents to prepare for your interview and possibly for further applications.

Chapter 6: Summary

Download the PD, job advertisement and other relevant documents

Get out your highlighter to mark key words and phrases and your examples – print and keep this list near your computer for easy reference

Read the PD instructions carefully

Open the résumé template

Proofread your résumé – download the QUICK GUIDE to Proofreading. Print it and keep it near your computer for easy reference

Check your résumé against the PD using Jobscan or similar software – adjust your résumé in line with results to achieve an 80% ranking.

Write your Cover Letter using the COVER LETTER QUICK GUIDE- print it out and keep near your computer for easy reference

Update your LinkedIn Profile

Finalise and send off your application

Keep a copy of each application for easy reference when you get an interview or for your next application

Chapter 7

How to write a winner cover letter using a proven formula

Always provide a cover letter with your application, even if you complete an online form. It's another chance to 'sell' yourself to the human reader who will decide whether or not to offer you an interview. The purpose of the letter is to show the employer or recruiter how well you match the requirements of the job. You do this by highlighting your achievements that are relevant to the role. Be specific using facts and figures. Get the PD where you have highlighted key words and phrases. Make sure your cover letter matches what you have said in your résumé.

Here are a few tips to write a 'winner' cover letter for your application:

1. Check the accuracy of names, phone numbers and email addresses.

2. Put the address of the organisation at the top left of your letter.

3. Put the date under the address

4. Put the job title and vacancy reference number and under the date. e.g.
RE Position: Administration Officer REF: 12345

5. Find out the name of the person who will be reading your application and personally address your letter – check you have the correct spelling and title. If you don't know the person's name, use 'Good morning' as the greeting – not 'Dear Sir or Madam' or 'To whom it may concern'.

6. Highlight key words and phrases to use in your letter.

7. First paragraph – state where and when you saw the advert and the reason for the letter.

8. Second paragraph - state how you 'match' the requirements of the position and link your qualifications, skills and experience to the requirements of the job.

9. Third paragraph - highlight a few key achievements that relate to this role

10. Use third person referrals from appraisals, clients' comments, etc. to build credibility and 'SELL' your claims.

11. Keep the letter to one page in length and use the same font and point size (e.g. Calibri 11 point) in your letter and résumé so that you have consistent 'branding'.

12. Finish with a strong close, as if you expect to be selected for an interview.

13. Type your name and supply your digital signature if you are able to do so.

14. Add enc. at the bottom of your letter. This means 'enclosure' and is used if you are adding other documentation such as a résumé and other documentation.

How to write your cover letter using a proven formula

Fig 7.0 Cover Letter Proven Formula

Example of completed cover letter for Administrative Officer role

Sarah Sample
Somewhere, QLD 4223
Telephone: 0000 000 000
Email: sarah.sample@gmail.com

Ms Robyn Rickard
Business Development Officer
ABC High School
Somewhere, QLD

15 January 2017

POSITION: ADMINISTRATIVE OFFICER (GENERIC)
JOB AD REF: SER22760/16

Good morning Robyn,

I'd like to express my interest in the advertised position of Administrative Officer (Generic) at DEF State High School. I am passionate about helping students achieve their goals and would love to work in an environment where I can make a difference to students and their families.

With 25 years' experience in administrative support/PA roles, I believe I have the experience and capability to provide high level administrative support to the Principal and Business Services Manager. I am dedicated to helping children learn as evidenced by my recent completion of Certificate 111 in Education Support and my voluntary assistance with reading and maths programs at ABC State School.

I also have a Blue Card, First Aid Certificate and Working with Children Card. I would be delighted to take on the additional role of nominated First Aid Officer for the school.

I'm confident that I have the skills and experience to provide high level support to the principal and other staff and build close relationships with students and their families. I believe I have the specialised knowledge, initiative and judgement to perform this role to a high standard.

I look forward to meeting with you to discuss this position in person.

Regards

Sarah Sample

Sarah Sample

Fig 7.1 Completed Cover Letter for Administrative Officer Role

Example of completed cover letter showing key words

Sarah Sample
Somewhere, QLD 4223
Telephone: 0000 000 000
Email: sarah.sample@gmail.com

Ms Robyn Rickard
Business Development Officer
ABC High School
Somewhere, QLD

15 January 2017

POSITION: ADMINISTRATIVE OFFICER (GENERIC)
JOB AD REF: SER22760/16

Good morning Robyn,

I'd like to express my interest in the advertised position of Administrative Officer (Generic) at DEF State High School. I am passionate about helping students achieve their goals and would love to work in an environment where I can make a difference to students and their families.

With 25 years' experience in administrative support/PA roles, I believe I have the experience and capability to provide high level administrative support to the Principal and Business Services Manager. I am dedicated to helping children learn as evidenced by my recent completion of Certificate 111 in Education Support and my voluntary assistance with reading and maths programs at ABC State School.

I also have a Blue Card, First Aid Certificate and Working with Children Card. I would be delighted to take on the additional role of nominated First Aid Officer for the school.

I'm confident that I have the skills and experience to provide high level support to the principal and other staff and build close relationships with students and their families. I believe I have the specialised knowledge, initiative and judgement to perform this role to a high standard.

I look forward to meeting with you to discuss this position in person.

Regards

Sarah Sample

Sarah Sample
Enc.

Fig 7.2 Cover Letter showing key words

Chapter 7: Summary

Always provide a cover letter with your application, even if you complete an online form. It's another chance to 'sell' yourself to the human reader who will decide whether or not to offer you an interview.

Never simply copy and paste the name and address of a new organisation to your standard cover letter. You need to add key words relevant to this role and address it personally.

Check the accuracy of names, phone numbers and email addresses in your letter. Make sure your voicemail message and email address are professional.

Never address the recipient as 'Dear Sir or Madam' or 'To Whom It May Concern' – try to find the name of the person who will be reading applications and personally address the letter.

Keep the letter to one page in length and use the same font and point size (e.g. Calibri 11 point) in your letter and résumé so that you have consistent 'branding'.

Finish with a strong close, as if you expect to be selected for an interview.

Chapter 8

QUICK PROOFREADING GUIDE – 14 Points to ensure your application moves to the 'YES' pile

We often see what we want to see, not what we've really written. Proofreading is one of the most important parts of your job application, so take the time to get it right. It only takes one or two errors to ruin your chance of being selected for an interview. Recruiters state that the most common errors they find are spelling, grammar, typos and incorrect use of common words (homonyms), where the words sound the same but have a different meaning e.g. 'there', 'they're' and 'their'. We've developed a cheat sheet to help you with these words. You can print it out from the link in the Resources for Career Changers section

14 Point Proofreading Guide
1. Get some fresh air before you start.
So, you've finished your application and you're keen to hit the 'send' button on your computer. Don't do it! Let your application 'sit' for a few hours (or better yet a few days). This enables you to see it with 'fresh eyes' when you proofread. You'll be amazed at the silly errors you've made.

2. Print a hard copy of your application for proofreading.
It's easier to identify errors on a printed page than on a computer screen, so always print out a completed hard copy to proofread.

3. Avoid fluorescent lighting when proofreading.
The flicker rate of fluoro lights is slower than standard lighting, making it more difficult to pick up errors. Use strong natural light where possible – preferably away from the room where you wrote your application — so that you'll get a fresh perspective.

4. Run the spell checker and the grammar checker.
This is a first line of defence only – don't rely on it to do all of the work for you.

5. Edit for content, structure and marketing appeal.
Make sure the facts flow in a logical, chronological sequence.
Use workplace examples that demonstrate your skills and abilities
Use present tense for current positions and past tense for former positions.
'Sell' your achievements through quotes from written references, appraisals, etc.
Make sure info in your résumé (periods of employment, achievements, etc.) matches info in your selection criteria statement if you are applying for a government job
Make sure your application looks professional with consistent formatting

6. Use the KISS Principle – Keep It Simple Sweetheart

Check that you have used short words, short sentences, short paragraphs and bullet points to make your application dynamic and easy to read. You only have 6 seconds to impress the reader.

7. Look for words that sound the same but have different meanings.

There are many words that sound the same, but have different meanings. These are called homonyms. They aren't picked up by spell checkers and grammar checkers, so you need to be aware of the differences in meanings. For example, use 'there' – 'over *there* in the shade'- when you are talking about a place and use *their* when you are referring to ownership – *their hats*. Use *they're* when you mean *they are*. Please see following CHEAT SHEET, which is also in the Resources for Career Changers.

8. Double check titles, names, addresses, phone numbers and reference numbers for accuracy.

Employers and recruiters get upset if their names are misspelled. Wouldn't you? Make sure you check titles, names, phone numbers, mobile numbers, email addresses, postal addresses and the vacancy reference number.

9. Check for padding and eliminate redundant words and phrases.

Aim to remove 10 to 20 per cent of what you've written to make your application punchy. Get out your red pen and remove anything that isn't absolutely essential.

10. Use active voice – not passive voice.

Passive voice slows down the reading and gives an impersonal tone to your application. An example of passive voice is: 'Tweety was eaten by Sylvester' and the active voice is: 'Sylvester ate Tweety.' Poor Tweety loses no matter which voice you use, but your application will move along faster with active voice.

11. Double check little words: 'and', 'or', 'of', 'it', and 'is' for typos.

It's very easy to repeat these little words without meaning to, so read backwards to see if you have doubled up.

12. Check for your own 'common errors'.

Most people make a few mistakes on a regular basis. It might be the word 'manager' written as 'manger' or it might be *applicaition* instead of *application*. Another very common error is 'form' instead of 'from'. The spelling checker won't necessarily see these words as incorrect so make a list of your common errors to check for yourself.

13. Proofread for one type of error at a time.

It's easy to get distracted while proofreading, especially after writing an application that is more exhausting than running a marathon. Read through your application for each of your common errors separately. For example, start with spelling and grammar, then check through for incorrect use of homonyms, apostrophes, verb tenses, and so on.

14. Go over your application one last time using techniques that work for you.

Read your application silently. 'Look' for mistakes. Read your application out loud. 'Listen' for mistakes. Point with your finger to read one word at a time. Use a screen (a blank sheet of paper to cover the material not yet proofed). Read it backwards to focus on spelling and repetition of words, such as 'and and'.

15. Ask a friend with good written skills to proofread your application.

This is one of the best methods of proofreading. When you check your own work, you tend to see what you intended to write, rather than what you actually wrote. A friend will see what is actually there. (Make sure your friend has good written skills.

Beware of homonyms that can sink your chances of success

One of the pet peeves of recruiters and employers is seeing mistakes in job applications. One of the worst mistakes is using the wrong word when two or even three words sound the same, but have different meanings. These words are called homonyms.

Keep this handy CHEAT SHEET nearby so that you don't make mistakes in your business communication. Please see the "Resources for Career Changers" for instructions on how to access a downloadable copy of this Cheat Sheet.

If you've ever had trouble working out which word to use in your emails, reports and other communication, you've come to the right place. How many of the five sentences that follow are correct?

1. I had to pay a lot for *excess* luggage when I flew to Melbourne.
2. To *access* the flight lounge, I had to go past the main terminal.
3. *They're* not coming to the conference because *their* on leave.
4. *Their* going to miss the flight because they left *there* passports at home.
5. This bag is much *to* heavy for me. I have *too* bags altogether.

1. Correct
2. Correct
3. Incorrect *They're* not coming to the conference because *they're* on leave
4. Incorrect *They're* going to miss the flight because they forgot *their* passports.
5. Incorrect This bag is much *too* heavy for me. I have *two* bags altogether.

Word	Definition	Correct	Incorrect
Accept	A verb meaning 'to take or receive'	I *accept* responsibility for sales.	I *except* responsibility for sales.
Except	Usually a preposition meaning 'excluding'	I did all the jobs *except* the filing.	I did all the jobs *accept* the filing.
Tip: If you want to *exclude* someone or something, use *except*. Otherwise, use *accept*.			
Bought	Past tense of the verb 'to buy'	I *bought* a new outfit to wear to the interview	I *brought* a new outfit to wear to the interview.
Brought	Past tense of the verb 'to bring'	I *brought* some work samples to the interview with me.	I *bought* some work samples to the interview with me.
Tip: If you had to carry it, use 'brought'. If you had to pay for it, use 'bought'.			
Its	Possessive form of 'it'	The cat shook its fur.	The cat shook it's fur.
It's	A contraction of 'it is'	*It's* Monday morning.	*Its* Monday morning.
Tip: An easy way to remember this is if you can insert it is, you should use it's.			
Than	Used in comparisons.	I like red better *than* blue.	She is nicer *then* he.
Then	Indication of point in time; alternatively can mean 'also', or 'next'.	First I will go to the store. *Then* I will go to the beach.	I will *than* go to the store.
Tip: If you're comparing two things, use 'than'. If you're talking about time, use 'then'			
There	Opposite of 'here' meaning 'in or at that place'.	*There* (a place) is the field.	*Their* is the field.
They're	Contraction of 'they' and 'are'.	I hope *they're* (they are) coming.	I hope *there* coming.
Tip: Use they're when you can replace the word with the phrase they are. The word there relates to a place ('here' is in the word 'there'). If neither of these fit, or if the word is followed by a noun, you should probably use 'their'.			

Fig. 8.0 Cheat Sheet – Homonyms That Can Sink Your Chances of Success

Chapter 8: Summary

Let your application 'sit for a while so that you can see it with fresh eyes.

Print it out and read it in strong natural light if possible.

Edit for one thing at a time – grammar, typos, punctuation, homonyms, etc.

Double check titles, names, addresses, phone numbers and reference numbers for accuracy.

Ask a friend with good literacy skills to read it for you.

Look for mistakes that you commonly make such as miss-spelling certain words (manger for manager).

Read your application out loud – you'll often 'hear' a mistake that you missed 'seeing'.

Check the Homonyms Cheat Sheet regarding words that you confuse.

Chapter 9

QUICK GUIDE (LINKEDIN PROFILE) – how to build your brand (you and your skills) on social media

When you think of a brand, you think about their corporate colours, logo and slogan (branding statement). This is known as the 'personality of the brand'.

For example, Kelloggs markets itself as the *Breakfast of Champions* using surf lifesavers and other healthy 'champions' as the face of the brand. Their website shows commitment to helping provide breakfasts for children in low socio-economic areas. How would you feel if a Kellogg's CEO was caught drink-driving? Would it affect the brand in your eyes? Yes!

Similarly, your résumé is your marketing document that has the job of 'selling' you (your brand) to a prospective employer. Your résumé may look professional, but how professional is your Linkedin Profile and posts on social media? A few inappropriate photos could finish your career before it starts.

Hays Career Advice states: *'Companies want to make sure prospective employees are a cultural fit, as well as having the right competencies. Social media makes it easier for employers and potential managers to check you out online so it is imperative that you take control and actively create and manage your personal brand online and offline.'*

Building your LinkedIn profile

LinkedIn is an important tool for job seeking and business people alike. An increasing number of companies and individuals are using the site to find candidates, post jobs and accept applications directly, and, because companies and buyers want to get to know someone before they hire or engage them, they will use it to informally vet candidates or providers.

While your résumé shows you can perform the competencies of the job, prospective employers will automatically check out your profile on LinkedIn to see how you 'fit' with other aspects of the job.

Your LinkedIn profile should not be a mirror image of your résumé, but it should complement it, show your personality, and tell your story in a way your résumé can't.

Did you know that the average person spends 8.5 seconds scanning a LinkedIn profile? That's a whole 2.5 seconds LONGER than they spend looking at your résumé!

So, how's your LinkedIn profile looking?

While it's the job of your résumé to convince an employer you've got the skills to do the job, it's the job of your LinkedIn profile to tell your professional 'story'. Your profile should talk about who you are, and put a human face to your applications. Make sure the photo you use on your profile is professional – forget about looking cool in your boardies.

LinkedIn is an important tool for job seeking with many employers using LinkedIn to search for candidates and make direct approaches, post jobs and accept applications directly. They also use it to informally screen potential employees and shortlisted candidates. Remember you are judged by the company you keep, so choose your connections wisely.

A recent social recruiting survey found that 80% of hiring companies use LinkedIn for recruiting purposes, so you need to make sure you project the right image.

10 Tips to build your brand and 'sell' yourself on LinkedIn:

1. DON'T just copy your résumé onto your LinkedIn profile
Your résumé is a concise, factual account of your career history to date, while LinkedIn enables you to show prospective employers your personality and relationships with employers, clients and others. Never just copy your résumé on to your LinkedIn profile – even for a short time.

2. Make sure you have a customised URL
Your LinkedIn profile also needs to be keyword rich and have a customised URL so you can be found in searches beyond LinkedIn. Make it easy for employers to contact you.

Example: www.linkedin.com/pub/smith-mary/1/a5/539/

3. Choose a strong headline, not your Job Title
Most people think they should use their Job Title as the headline on their LinkedIn Profile. How dull! In copywriting, the headline 'hooks' the reader and makes them want to read more. Readers spend about 5 seconds reading a page, so if your headline doesn't 'grab' them, it's all over. Advertising guru, John Caples, states: *If I had a week to write an ad, I'd spend the 6 days on the headline and one on the copy.* The best headlines contain benefits for the reader and are based on self-interest, news curiosity or a quick and easy way to do something.

You need to maximise the 120 characters allowed in your headline by describing what you can do for your reader. Compare the two headlines below.

Allan Brown

CEO; Business Strategist
XYZ Professional Coaching Company

Connect with Allan   Send Allan Inmail   500 +

Fig. 9.0 Example of 'Ho Hum' Branding Slogan

Allan Brown

I've helped 7 Companies reach $1 Billion. Who wants to be #8?
XYZ Professional Coaching Company

Connect with Allan   Send Allan Inmail   500 +

Fig. 9.1 Example of branding slogan that shakes the rafters with benefits for the reader

Allan Brown has taken control of his own brand, connected with his audience and 'sold' himself, as well as his work. This is a powerful branding strategy. Would you like to be #8?

4. Write a Summary that tells your story

This 2,000-character space is where the LinkedIn algorithm searches for key words, so be sure to fill it with information to interest your target audience. It's a great opportunity to attach videos, seminars, published materials or anything else that shows what you can do for your clients. Make sure you include industry key words and key words from jobs you've applied for so that the robots will find you.

The Summary is NOT another version of your résumé. It's a short version of what you do and why you do it. From the example above, there's no doubt about what Bryan Franklin does for his clients. It's not enough these days to expect your experience to speak for itself. You need to be your own Public Relations Specialist (Brand Ambassador) and you need to ensure that your professional online profile is interesting, engaging and full of information.

Take note. Always write in the first person e.g. 'I've helped', not the third person 'John has helped'. Using the third person makes you look pompous and out of touch with reality.

Example of a brilliant Summary that tells a story for the founder of Passion Point Framework:

 SUMMARY

"Harriet the Spy" was my Bible when I was a little girl. I copied her by spying on my neighbors and writing down what I observed in a little notebook, as well as noting questions that their behaviors triggered. I even spent a summer eating nothing but tomato sandwiches.

Today, I still "spy" on people, although these days, respondents give me their permission me to ask them nosy questions and pry into their homes.

My passion is inventing new, more powerful and profitable ways to listen creatively to consumers... and then turning the insights that emerge into business ideas that generate $50MM in annual revenue and above.

Our Passion Point Framework shows brands how to align with consumers' passions. These clients no longer have to settle for incremental growth, they enjoy exponential growth.

Send an email to kay@energyannex.com to learn more.

Specialties: Consumer Packaged Goods, B2B, pharmaceuticals, social media research, BRIC, qualitative market research, innovation, consumer insights

Fig. 9.2 Example of creative Linked In summary that tells a story and engages the reader

5. Show a multi-media view of your experience
Choose appropriate videos, training sessions, slide share presentations, YouTube videos, blogs, MP3s, webinars, photos, articles and other media that show a different side of you and your work from your résumé. When you mention your career, make sure you 'sell' what you have achieved in roles for each organisation. You can list key projects and show videos of those projects if appropriate.

6. Expand your social media presence
Join forums and groups related to your industry. Participate and share your knowledge. This builds credibility that you are an expert in this field. Share your updates on LinkedIn and click the box with the Twitter icon, followed by 'Share'.

7. Ask for Recommendations
Get up to two recommendations for each of your most important former positions. Preferably, obtain recommendations from people influential in your industry. Ask them to comment about certain aspects of you or your business, such as: 'How did you benefit from the training courses I developed for you? Were you happy with the outcomes? Would you recommend my service to other people needing assistance? Why?

8. Ask for Endorsements

Most of us hate to ask for endorsements. But, LinkedIn makes it easy to use the *Marketing Law of Reciprocity*. This means that if you endorse or recommend other people, they will generally reciprocate by endorsing or recommending you. So, start the ball rolling by endorsing other people in your group. Get as many quality endorsements as you can to show people reading your profile what you have achieved for others. People tend to believe what other people say – this is the basis for marketing endorsements such as Lifesavers recommending Nutri Grain – and it works for career changers in the same way.

9. Make sure your Profile is 100% complete.

If you want to be found by recruiters, having the relevant key words in the right places is important. Don't leave any blanks in your profile.

If your LinkedIn Profile is not 100% complete, LinkedIn penalizes you by lowering your search rank, ignoring your keywords and making you invisible.

10. Use Key Words in your profile

The LinkedIn algorithm looks for Keywords such as: Name, Headline, Company Name, Job Title and Skills. If employers don't have access to 'LinkedIn Recruiter', they use 'LinkedIn search'. 'LinkedIn search' is 'personalized', which means it provides search results that are unique to the searcher and based mainly on 'relevance' to your network (showing your 1st, 2nd and 3rd degree connections when you search)

Chapter 9: Summary

Employers spend 8.5 seconds scanning a LinkedIn profile, compared to just 6 seconds looking at a résumé – make it count!

A recent social recruiting survey found that 80% of hiring companies use LinkedIn for recruiting purposes, so you need to make sure you project the right image.

You need to maximise the 120 characters allowed in your headline by describing what you can do for your reader. Use benefits for the reader in your headline.

Use the 2000 words allowed in your summary to tell your story. Attach videos, seminars, published materials or anything else that shows what you can do for your clients.

Make sure you include industry key words and key words from jobs you've applied for so that the robots will find you.

Be active on Linkedin – provide endorsements and recommendations for others and they will usually do the same for you.

Join Linkedin groups related to your industry and participate fully to build your credibility as an expert in this field.

Make sure your Linkedin Profile is 100% complete otherwise LinkedIn will penalise you by lowering your search rank, ignoring your keywords and making you invisible.

Chapter 10

Tips on answering selection criteria for government jobs

To get a government job in Australia (and possibly in other countries), you generally have to jump through hoops called Selection Criteria (SC) which are now called 'Key Capabilities'.

Under the Public Sector Capability Framework (PSCF), applicants need to address the selection criteria (key capabilities) either by submitting a written statement against the selection criteria (the current method) or by providing sufficient detail in their cover letter and résumé to show how they meet the criteria.

Trends in government employment

They also need to meet word limits on their responses. For example, if the applicant chooses to write a selection criteria statement, the suggested word limit is 300 words per criterion; if the applicant chooses to provide a résumé and cover letter, the suggested length is one page for the cover letter and three pages for the résumé. This may vary widely depending on the job and the organisation.

This makes it challenging for applicants to fit a four part response (STAR) into so few words. STAR stands for Situation, Task, Action and Result and is the standard format required for responses to selection criteria.

Over the past decade, jobs for people with a Certificate IV or higher have accounted for 43% of total employment growth, and this trend will continue. Job opportunities for workers with a bachelor degree or higher are increasing. Over the past three years, one out of every three new jobs created was for an employee with a bachelor degree or higher.

So, if you are thinking about applying for a government job, you can start by reading 'Get That Government Job' or 'Selection Criteria Toolkit'. Both are available through local libraries and online.

Here's an excerpt from an article by Ann Villiers called *'Selection Panel Secrets: How We Read Your Selection Criteria'*

http://selectioncriteria.com.au/governmentselectionpanelsecrets.shtml?mc_cid=c4725de03e&mc_eid=4e9e0b55d5

'I've have been sitting on government selection panels since 2003. This has not been an every now and then occurrence – it is my job to sit on selection panels, it's all I do! Not

only has this given me a great insight into how applicants approach their job applications, but also how selection panels assess these applications.

Panels want to put you in the 'no' pile. *A recruitment exercise is about finding the best person for the job, and selection panels want to do this as quickly and as easily as possible. One piece of insider information you may not know, is that seasoned panels are looking for reasons to eliminate you'.*

Well, that's certainly pretty brutal, but really shows the pressure that the panel are under to 'cull' the large number of applicants into a manageable number.

At present, Applicant Tracking Systems aren't used for government job applications, but it is absolutely essential to use key words and phrases from the PD to get short-listed for an interview.

Getting past 'human readers' is just as tough as getting past 'robot readers' looking for key words. So, you see how important it is to check and double check your application and make sure you have left no doubt whatsoever in the recruiter's mind. It might be worth referring back to *'How to sell yourself in your application'* as you write your statement.

Quick Introduction to writing a government application:

1. Download all of the documents and analyse them to see if you can provide actual examples for each criterion (Capability Statement). If you can't provide workplace examples, there's no point in proceeding with your application.

2. Call the 'contact person' on the PD to get answers to any questions you may have about the role. A good question to ask is: 'Is there someone acting in this position at the moment?' If there is, your chances are lowered because the person in the job can provide actual examples related to the job. You may decide it's not worth taking the time to write an application.

3. If you decide to proceed, highlight key words in the PD.

4. Note workplace examples of where you meet the requirements of the PD.

5. Write your responses to the SC (key Capabilities) using the STAR format.

6. Set up your document by writing the selection criteria and highlighting or bolding it and then writing your responses underneath. Make sure you include the position title, reference number and your contact details on the first page.

7. Use the STAR method when writing your responses.
S: Situation; T: Tasks; A: Actions; and R: Results.
Example:
 (S) In my role as Sales Manager at XYZ,
 (T) I was tasked with finding a solution to the problem of excessive customer

complaints. (A) I conducted a survey of stakeholders and found that a high percentage of them were upset about a new initiative the company had employed. I spoke to relevant groups and persuaded management to change the policy in line with my findings.

(R) The result was an improved situation and resultant 33% increase in sales over the next 5 months.

8. Use quotes from appraisals and client testimonials to 'sell' yourself. State what you have achieved for former employers – use specific information such as % increases or decreases, savings, production improvements, etc.

9. Make sure you follow instructions in the PD. Usually, you will need to submit an online application. Try to download the application before you fill it in online. It will save you a lot of problems with writing in little square boxes and not being able to see what you have already written.

10. Choose your referees wisely – make sure you have referees who can comment on your work performance in relation to this role, not personal referees. These have no bearing on a reference for employment. Most jobs require your current supervisor as a referee – if this is a confidentiality issue, you can explain it in your application.

Please see the Selection Criteria Statement for the advertised role of Administrative Officer in a school environment that follows.

Examples of responses to selection criteria

Selection criteria: Able to operate effectively in a team, contributing positively to team operations and working relationships

In my current role as a Sales Trainer, I have worked as part of a team for the past nine years and understand the importance of great teamwork. As a team member, I am mindful of my role and the roles of others to ensure successful outcomes in working with clients and internal customers. I often participate in brainstorming sessions and generate Action Plans for the organisation.

For example, we recently received customer complaints about a new product we were offering. I discussed the problems with my team and organised a focus group of customers to explore the cause of their complaints. I then briefed my team on the findings and wrote reports to management, offering suggestions for fixing the problem and rebuilding the relationships with clients. These suggestions were adopted nationally and team sales have increased by 11% in the past 3 months following my intervention.

Selection criteria: Demonstrated client service focus in a client service environment

For the last five years, I have been working with FSG Finance as a customer service officer. My job involves direct client contact on a daily basis and I am often the first point of contact for clients. I am proactive in my relationship with clients and have established a loyal client base in my local community. This involves a regular calling program to talk to clients about any needs they may have and meeting with them face-to-face to resolve any problems.

For example, an elderly customer enquired about her bank account as she felt that there was a discrepancy in the balance. After having a conversation with her in the privacy of my office, I discovered that what was really concerning her was the amount of her last pension payment. As she was not comfortable contacting Centrelink, I did so on her behalf and we were able to clarify the issue and resolve the problem. She was most appreciative of my help and left my office very happy with the outcome. I am passionate and committed to providing excellent client service and undertake regular training in customer feedback, customer relations and conflict resolution as provided by my employer. I am confident in handling any situation that may arise and will always go 'the extra mile' with my service.

Selection criteria: Awareness of Occupational Health & Safety Issues (OH&S)

My current workplace has a clear, defined and well-constructed occupational health and safety (OH&S) policy framework. Each employee is responsible for the safety and wellbeing of themselves and others. All work is performed in accordance with the requirements of the health and safety policy and procedures. I have undertaken annual training in all facets of safe work practices including manual handling, correct workstation set-up, risk and hazard identification and the reporting of all accidents or incidents. The company conducts an OH&S self audit every three months and all team members share the responsibility of this audit. We identify risks and hazards and find strategies to deal with these appropriately.

For example, I identified that the workstations of several employees were not compliant with a safe working environment. I arranged for a meeting with the OH&S consultant to discuss these issues. The workstations were adjusted to ensure optimum health and safety outcomes for staff.

Selection criteria: Ability to use information technology in a school setting

As part of my degree program at XYZ University, I completed numerous projects that required me to source information, verify the origins and analyse the implications. I used various technologies to undertake these tasks including the Internet, online library databases, and even microfiche. I am adept in all Microsoft Office software and InDesign software.

In my role as a Business Development Officer at ABC School, I was tasked with managing fund-raising projects. When I started at the school, there was no appropriate data management system that I could use to manage the numerous fundraising projects.

I developed a database to manage the contact information for all sponsors, which also included records of when and why they were contacted, what the sponsorships agreement comprised and how it would be delivered. I managed this system throughout the project and ensured that it streamlined communication and information sharing amongst the project team members.

My initiative resulted in a streamlining of effort with no double handling, a clear record of activities undertaken and a database for future use for fundraising efforts. I was commended for my initiative and competence in information technology systems.

Selection criteria: Demonstrated ability to meet strict guidelines and determine and allocate work priorities under direction and in a dynamic environment, including the ability to maintain confidentiality.

Currently, I organise rosters for one full time staff member and three part time staff members. I allocate work priorities in line with expected peaks and troughs in sales, based on projected sales. I am aware of confidentiality issues, particularly in relation to the Privacy Act and ensure customer information is stored securely and is available only to staff members who are authorised to access it. I maintain customer records in line with the requirements of the Australian Tax Office and keep records of repairs for warranty purposes for two years. All records are then shredded to ensure client confidentiality.

I have ten years' experience in the retail industry. In this period, I have been a member of a sales team and reported regularly to a Sales Manager, participated in group discussions and was involved in store training. I enjoy being a member of a productive team and am able to build strong working relationships based on mutual respect and co-operation. I support quality human resource management practices such as equal employment opportunity, anti-discrimination, ethical behaviour and ensure safe work practices.

Proven ability to prioritise my time and meet organisational deadlines such as paying Superannuation each month and PAYG every three months. I have set up separate bank accounts to ensure money is available when required.

My ability to prioritise workloads is further demonstrated through successfully combining running a business (which won the Quest Business Achiever Awards three times) with undertaking tertiary study. This has involved allocating time for research, completion of assignments, attending lectures, conducting meetings with suppliers, opening the store for extended retail shopping hours, covering for staff when absent due to illness, etc.

I am confident that these examples demonstrate my ability to meet the above criterion.

Selection criteria: Demonstrated substantial experience in coordinating, developing, implementing and evaluating community safety and crime prevention advice, planning strategies and policy documents.

In various roles within XYZ Police, I gained substantial experience in coordinating, developing, implementing and evaluating community safety and crime prevention advice, strategic planning strategies and policy documents.

As Policy Officer in Corporate Policy in XYZ Police, I provided policy and procedural advice to police and public service employees. I also developed policies through consultation with both internal and external stakeholders. My key role was to assess policy change requests in accordance with the police development framework and to liaise with departmental, regional and divisional stakeholders to present reports and ensure policy changes addressed all potential risks. I also communicated policy changes to staff on the intranet.

The outcome was that I was recognised for my efforts and promoted twice for my operational knowledge of policing issues than amended policy to improve outcomes for operational police.

Selection criteria: Capacity for leadership in education within the context of Education XYB's strategic plan.

In my roles within Education XYB as Acting Deputy Principal and Curriculum Support Teacher at Ashgrove Outdoor Education Centre, I have demonstrated my capacity for leadership in education within the context of Education Queensland's strategic plan through:

Developing and implementing Adventure Based Programs for behaviourally challenged 13-15 year old students

Developing certified quality work programs, work units, student resource packages, and assessment instruments in the areas of junior science, junior and senior mathematics and senior biology.

I have been commended and promoted to Deputy Principal based on my performance in this role.

Example of school Administration Officer Selection Criteria Statement:

SARAH SAMPLE

Somewhere, QLD 4223   Email: sarah.sample@gmail.com   Phone: 0000 000 000

Administrative Officer (Generic)   SER227602/16

Key Capability 1: Supports strategic direction

Demonstrated knowledge or ability to rapidly acquire knowledge of departmental administrative policies, practices and procedures used in schools, including relevant student and financial software/programs.

I have 25 years experience in diverse industries where I have consistently supported the strategic direction of each organisation where I was employed.

I have recently completed and passed all 17 units of *Certificate III in Education Support* and have an up-to-date understanding of administrative policies, practices and procedures used in schools. Whilst I have not used any school software programs, I have quickly learned other specialist software programs in my former roles in finance, hospitality, training and legal and accounting services. These included MYOB, Starfleet, EzyRez and Navision. When I commenced my accounts/payroll role at Cullen Bay Resorts they were in the process of changing software programs. Accordingly, I had to learn both programs simultaneously and quickly in order fulfil my role.

In my role as Administrative Assistant at IS Australia in Darwin, I assisted in the preparation of documentation relating to training, policies and strategies that complied with the Australian Training Framework (ATF) and supported the organisation's strategic direction.

I believe these examples demonstrate how I have positively supported strategic direction in previous positions.

Key Capability 2: Achieves results

Demonstrated administrative, keyboard and word processing skills and an ability to work independently and/or with limited supervision.

I possess 25 years' experience in various administrative roles including reception, legal secretary, personal assistant and accounts payable and receivable. I have worked as part of a team and also in situations where I was the only administrative member of staff.

I've completed an advanced secretarial course and am proficient in all areas of administration. When last tested, my typing speed was 75wpm with 100% accuracy.

An example of how I have achieved results for previous organisations is in my role at ABC Resorts. When I joined them, they were in debt for $200,000. I introduced new systems and worked closely with clients in debt, working out payment plans. The result was zero debt when I left.

Another example of my ability to achieve results is in my role of Personal Assistant to the Sales and Marketing Manager at Kendall Australasia. Based on the outstanding results I achieved and my ability to develop and maintain strong relationships with clients and customers, I was promoted to National Marketing Coordinator.

Fig. 10.0 Key Capabilities Statement for Administrative Officer role

Key Capability 3: Supports productive working relationships

Ability to build and sustain positive working relationships while providing prompt and courteous service to clients.

I enjoy establishing good working relationships with both colleagues and clients and am able to get along with all personalities. I am passionate about providing exceptional customer service and am always willing to go the extra mile to assist clients or solve problems. I make a point of remembering personal details about each client in order to make them feel valued. An example of this is in my cleaning business, where I have worked with a wide range of clients. One of these clients has an adult daughter with a dual disability that makes her fearful of new people in the home. I have developed a very close relationship with this young woman and her family and her mother has offered to be a referee for this application.

Over the last few years in my voluntary role as a support reading and maths tutor at Currumbin State School where my children attend, and also whilst doing my vocational placement for my Certificate III in Education Support, I have developed strong working relationships with the teachers in the classes I assist. Two of these teachers have offered to be my referees.

Key Capability 4: Displays personal drive and integrity

Basic understanding of occupational health and safety, equal employment opportunity and anti-discriminatory practices and behaviour as applied in a work environment.

I have attended numerous OHS training programs and believe that OH&S legislation places the responsibility on both employers and employees at a workplace to ensure the health and safety of others. Employers are responsible for practical procedures that identify and manage exposure to risk in the workplace while employees must follow organisational policies and procedures for the safety of themselves and others.

When I relocated to Darwin, I accepted a short term contract with the government department *NT Power and Water*. Occupational Health and Safety was paramount to the organisation and I attended and recorded minutes of weekly meetings regarding these practices. Also, these topics were covered in great detail in the Education Support course I have recently completed.

I understand that the Equal Employment Opportunity (EEO) Act 1997 ensures that employees are recruited, selected and promoted on an equitable basis. EEO is based on merit based selection because it requires employees to be selected and promoted on the basis of their individual skills and abilities in relation to the requirements of the job and not on personal characteristics such as gender, age, race or nationality.

In all of my roles over the last 25 years, I have worked harmoniously with people from a range of ethnic backgrounds. I enjoy diversity and learn from everyone I meet. I also have utter respect for their individual beliefs and practices and abhor discrimination of any kind.

Key Capability 5: Communicates with influence

Demonstrated interpersonal and communication skills including the ability to work with all members of the school community both individually and as a member of a team.

In all of my former roles, I have demonstrated my ability to work as a member of a harmonious team and also to work independently to achieve organisational objectives. I am a 'people' person and love nothing more than working in a cohesive team to achieve corporate objectives. I've successfully worked independently in roles as a PA and Administration Assistant. My referees will verify my success in both team and independent roles.

My interpersonal and communication skills are shown through receptionist and liaison roles where I have built strong working relationships with clients, management and stakeholders.

Fig. 10.1 Key Capabilities Statement for Administrative Officer role

Chapter 10: Summary

When deciding if you should apply for the position, work out if you can supply actual workplace examples for each criterion. If you can't, you're wasting your time.

Use the STAR Method of Situation, Task, Action and Result so that your structure is succinct and easy to read.

Phone the contact person to find out as much as possible about the job, particularly if there is an acting person in the role. This may limit your chance of success.

Make sure you update your resume and LinkedIn Profile in line with te key words used in your Key Capability Statement.

Choose your referees wisely – make sure you have referees who can comment on your work performance in relation to this role. Most jobs require your current supervisor as a referee – if this is a confidentiality issue, make note of it on your application.

Chapter 11

Résumé Makeover for Administrative Officer role – 'Before' and 'After'

Sarah's résumé worked very well for her for the past ten years. Now, she isn't getting a single response to numerous job applications.

Does that sound familiar?

The rules for writing résumés have changed, along with the way résumés are processed by recruiters and employers. To be successful, you must write your résumé for both robot readers and human readers. Listed below are some of the reasons the phone isn't ringing to offer Sarah an interview.

The following examples can be downloaded. Please see the "Resources for Career Changers" section at the back of the book for instructions.

Sarah's Résumé 'Before the Makeover

SARAH SAMPLE - RESUME

PERSONAL INFORMATION

Name: Sarah SAMPLE

Address: Somewhere QLD 4223

Telephone: 0000 000 000

Date of Birth: 2nd May 1974

Driver's Licence: Queensland C Class

Marital Status: Married, 2 children

Interests: Reading, music, beach, cycling

Remove Personal Info – you only need your contact details

EDUCATION & TRAINING

Secondary school isn't important for a person with 20 years' experience, but the current study of Cert.111 in Education Support is relevant to this

Secondary: ABC High School - School Certificate, 1986

Tertiary: Currently completing Certificate III in
                   Education Support

                   Somewhere College of TAFE
                   - Advanced Secretarial Course, 1987

SKILLS

Current First Aid Certificate

Typing: 75wpm 100% accuracy

Software packages: Word
                   Excel
                   MYOB
                   Starfleet
                   EzyRez
                   Navision
                   PowerPoint
                   Outlook / Outlook Express
                   My Retail Assistant

Present this info in columns, along with other hard and soft skills

Don't leave so much blank white space in the layout – it's wasting the chance to 'sell' your skills to the employer

Fig. 11.0 Page 1 of 'Before' Résumé

Sarah's Résumé 'Before the Makeover

SARAH SAMPLE - RESUME

EMPLOYMENT HISTORY

March 2012 to Present
IST Australia (Brisbane)
Administration Officer – Quality and Compliance - part-time position

Change the way this info is presented to Name of company, Location, Your Position and Dates on right hand side

IS Australia is fully accredited RTO approved by the Australian Government to provide a comprehensive range of training and employment services.

Duties:
- ✓ Proof reading and formatting documentation relating to training, policies and strategies
- ✓ Preparation of training material for student log books
- ✓ Creation and upkeep of spreadsheets
- ✓ Assessing feedback from students and trainers
- ✓ General office duties

Use standard bullets, not fancy ones that may confuse robot scanners

June 2004 to March 2012
ABC Bay Resorts (Darwin)
Accounts / Payroll / PA

Cullen Bay Resorts consists of two towers comprising standard hotel rooms and one and two bedroom apartments owned by investors and operated under management rights.

Duties:
- ✓ Minimising debtors to achieve maximum cash flow
- ✓ Invoicing and processing payments
- ✓ Liaising and corresponding with apartment owners, corporate clients and industry representatives
- ✓ End of month procedures including owner statements
- ✓ Payroll
- ✓ Superannuation
- ✓ PA tasks for Director
- ✓ Marketing
- ✓ Accounts Payable
- ✓ Assist in reception in peak periods including guest check-in/out

Too many duties and no achievements

June 1998 – January 2004
ABC Management Pty Ltd (Sydney)
Personal Assistant to Managing Director

International Property development company employing 14 staff and various consulting companies.
Duties:
- ✓ Analysing and actioning correspondence and calls to MD
- ✓ Arranging meetings both locally and internationally
- ✓ Organising travel and accommodation arrangements
- ✓ Diary Management
- ✓ Preparation and organisation of documentation for overseas business trips
- ✓ Preparation and typing of correspondence and schedules including instigation of same
- ✓ Handling issues of confidential/personal/sensitive nature
- ✓ Management of personal accounts
- ✓ Office Management
- ✓ Liaising with consultants and representatives

Fig 11.1 Page 2 of the 'Before' Résumé

Do you have any of these mistakes on your résumé?

SARAH SAMPLE - RESUME

- ✓ Assisting on site employees
- ✓ Media monitoring
- ✓ Internet research

 Too many duties and no achievements

July 1994 - June 1998
ABC Australasia Pty Limited   (Sydney)
National Marketing Co-ordinator after merging with ABZ

This is a pharmaceutical company employing 40 staff.

Duties:
- ✓ Monthly sales analysis/preparation
- ✓ Wholesaler ranging
- ✓ New product co-ordinator
- ✓ Bonus/promotional activity   (preparation and monitoring)
- ✓ Wholesaler and representative support   (18 representatives nationally)
- ✓ Market trends/competitors/general trade activity - reporting
- ✓ Product analysis - turnover (individual and brand)
- ✓ Pharmacy support programme
    - data base contact
    - co-ordination
    - maintenance
    - development
- ✓ Advertising programme
    - co-ordination
    - maintenance
    - support to participants
- ✓ Monthly commissions

 Too many duties and no achievements

OTHER
Reading and Maths Assistance XYZ State School
Telebet Operator   Unitab (NT)
TAB operator   Flight terminals & Eureka terminals
Sales Assistant   Trackmaster Factory Store
Volunteer Cosmetic Care Worker for the Australian Red Cross

This info isn't really relevant, so leave it out

REFEREES

Ms Betty Brown   Mrs Doris Green
(ex) Quality Manager   Current client
ABC Company   Ph: 0000 000 000
Ph: 0000 000 000

Mr Brad Brown
(ex) General Manager – ABC Property Group
Ph: 0000 000 000

 Only include referees if you are specifically asked to do so.

If you do include referees, make sure you provide a current email address for each referee

Fig. 11.2 Page 3 of the 'Before' Résumé

Sarah's Résumé 'after' the Makeover

We've seen what doesn't work in the résumé above – now, let's have a look at what is working very well for career changers with our Résumé Makeover for the school role of Administrative Assistant. Sarah's résumé is now optimised and chock full of juicy key words to get the robots salivating. We'll show you the key words listed on the updated résumé a bit later.

This front page now contains the most important information to 'sell' the applicant's skills and experience. Note, we placed the applicant's Qualifications on the front page because they were important to the application and gave the applicant an advantage. Normally, they would be placed after the Employment section.

Instructions on how to download these documents are in the "Resources for Career Changers" section at the back of this book.

Here's page 1 'After' the makeover:

SARAH SAMPLE   Résumé

Somewhere, QLD 4223   Email: sarah.sample@gmail.com   Phone: 0000 000 000

Administrative Officer (Generic)   SER227602/16

PROFESSIONAL SUMMARY

Professional Administrative Officer with 25 years' experience in contributing to the efficient management and administration of companies and providing high level administrative support to management, including developing and maintaining financial/administrative systems and procedures, marketing, reception services, and daily communication with clients, suppliers and colleagues.

QUALIFICATIONS (CERTIFICATIONS)

Certificate III in Education Support   Current First Aid Certificate
Advanced Secretarial Course   Blue Card for Working with Children

PROFESSIONAL SKILLS

Keyboard Skills -Typing: 75wpm 100% accuracy   Typing of reports, minutes, newsletters
Computing Skills - Proficient in MYOB, MS Office   Correspondence - Incoming/outgoing mail
and numerous other software programs   Word processing and spreadsheet software
Processing orders and reconciling invoices   Stock control -ordering consumables
Taking minutes of meetings   Preparation of reports and prospectuses
Answering telephone enquiries   Liaising with clients and colleagues
High level customer service   OH&S compliance report preparation
Accounts payable & receivable, reconciliation   Diary management/organising meetings
Organising travel and accommodation arrangements   Managing confidential information

PROFESSIONAL EXPERIENCE

IST Australia (Brisbane, Qld)   **March 2012 to Present**
Administration Officer – Quality and Compliance (part-time position)
IST Australia is a fully accredited RTO approved by the Australian Government to provide a comprehensive range of training and employment services.

Duties:
- Proof reading and formatting documentation relating to training, policies and strategies
- Preparation of training material for student log books
- Creation and upkeep of spreadsheets
- Assessing feedback from students and trainers and converting into reports and graphs
- General office duties

Achievement:
Known as 'Eagle Eye' for my thorough proofreading of training materials, policies and procedures.

Fig. 11.3 Page 1 'After' the makeover

Here's page 2 'After' the makeover:

SARAH SAMPLE

Somewhere, QLD 4223   Email: sarah.sample@gmail.com   Phone: 0000 000 000

PROFESSIONAL EXPERIENCE (Continued)

ABC Bay Resorts (Darwin, Qld)   June 2004 to March 2012
Accounts / Payroll / PA
ABC Bay Resorts consists of two towers comprising standard hotel rooms and one and two bedroom
apartments owned by investors and operated under management rights.

Duties:
- Minimising debtors to achieve maximum cash flow; invoicing and processing payments
- Liaising and corresponding with apartment owners, corporate clients and industry representatives
- End of month procedures including owner statements
- Accounts Payable; Payroll; Superannuation
- Marketing
- Assist in reception in peak periods including guest check-in/check-out

Achievement:
Reduced debtors for Holiday Resort from over 200k upon starting role to zero when I left.

ABC Management Pty Ltd (Sydney, NSW)   June 1998 – June 2004
Personal Assistant to Managing Director
International Property Development company employing 14 staff and various consulting companies.

Duties:
- Analysing and actioning correspondence and calls to MD
- Arranging meetings both locally and internationally
- Organising travel and accommodation arrangements
- Diary Management
- Preparation and organisation of documentation for overseas business trips
- Preparation and typing of correspondence and schedules including instigation of same
- Handling issues of confidential/personal/sensitive nature

ABC Australasia Pty Limited   (Sydney, NSW)   July 1994 - June 1998
Personal Assistant to Sales and Marketing Manager
Promoted to National Marketing Co-ordinator after merging with ABZ
This is a pharmaceutical company employing 40 staff.

Duties:
- Monthly sales analysis/preparation/commissions for 18 staff
- New product co-ordinator
- Bonus/promotional activity   (preparation and monitoring)
- Wholesaler and representative support   (18 representatives nationally)
- Market trends/competitors/general trade activity - reporting
- Product analysis - turnover (individual and brand)
- Pharmacy support programme- data base contact; co-ordination; maintenance; development
- Advertising programme co-ordination; maintenance; support to participants

Achievement:
Promoted to National Marketing Manager based on development and implementation of innovative
marketing strategies that increased turnover by 33% in 12 months.

Fig 11.4 'After' the Makeover Page 2

Key Words shown on the front page of the makeover

SARAH SAMPLE

Résumé

Somewhere, QLD 4223   Email: sarah.sample@gmail.com   Phone: 0000 000 000

Administrative Officer (Generic)   SER227602/16

PROFESSIONAL SUMMARY

Professional Administrative Officer with 25 years' experience in contributing to the efficient management and administration of companies and providing high level administrative support to management, including developing and maintaining financial/administrative systems and procedures, marketing, reception services, and daily communication with clients, suppliers and colleagues.

QUALIFICATIONS (CERTIFICATIONS)

Certificate III in Education Support
Advanced Secretarial Course

Current First Aid Certificate
Blue Card for Working with Children

PROFESSIONAL SKILLS

Keyboard Skills -Typing: 75wpm 100% accuracy
Computing Skills - Proficient in MYOB, MS Office
and numerous other software programs
Processing orders and reconciling invoices
Taking minutes of meetings
Answering telephone enquiries
High level customer service
Accounts payable & receivable, reconciliation
Organising travel and accommodation arrangements

Typing of reports, minutes, newsletters
Correspondence - Incoming/outgoing mail
Word processing and spreadsheet software
Stock control -ordering consumables
Preparation of reports and prospectuses
Liaising with clients and colleagues
OH&S compliance report preparation
Diary management/organising meetings
Managing confidential information

PROFESSIONAL EXPERIENCE

IST Australia (Brisbane, Qld)   **March 2012 to Present**
Administration Officer – Quality and Compliance (part-time position)
IST Australia is a fully accredited RTO approved by the Australian Government to provide a comprehensive range of training and employment services.

Duties:
- Proof reading and formatting documentation relating to training, policies and strategies
- Preparation of training material for student log books
- Creation and upkeep of spreadsheets
- Assessing feedback from students and trainers and converting into reports and graphs
- Reception and general office duties

Achievement:
Known as 'Eagle Eye' for my thorough proofreading of training materials, policies and procedures.

Fi

g. 11.5 'After' version of the Makeover with Key Words highlighted (page 1)

Somewhere, QLD 4223   Email: sarah.sample@gmail.com   Phone: 0000 000 000

PROFESSIONAL EXPERIENCE (Continued)

ABC Bay Resorts (Darwin, Qld)   **June 2004 to March 2012**
Accounts / Payroll / PA
ABC Bay Resorts consists of two towers comprising standard hotel rooms and one and two bedroom apartments owned by investors and operated under management rights.

Duties:
- Minimising debtors to achieve maximum cash flow; invoicing and processing payments
- Liaising and corresponding with apartment owners, corporate clients and industry representatives
- End of month procedures including owner statements
- Accounts Payable; Payroll; Superannuation
- Marketing – maintenance of spreadsheets and data systems
- Assist in reception in peak periods including guest check-in/check-out

Achievement:
Reduced debtors for Holiday Resort from over 200k upon starting role to zero when I left.

ABC Management Pty Ltd (Sydney, NSW)   **June 1998 – June 2004**
Personal Assistant to Managing Director
International Property Development company employing 14 staff and various consulting companies.

Duties:
- Analysing and actioning correspondence and calls to MD
- Arranging meetings both locally and internationally
- Organising travel and accommodation arrangements
- Diary Management
- Preparation and organisation of documentation for overseas business trips
- Preparation and typing of correspondence and schedules including instigation of same
- Handling issues of confidential/personal/sensitive nature

ABC Australasia Pty Limited   (Sydney, NSW)   **July 1994 - June 1998**
Personal Assistant to Sales and Marketing Manager
Promoted to National Marketing Co-ordinator after merging with ABZ
This is a pharmaceutical company employing 40 staff.

Duties:
- Monthly sales analysis/preparation/commissions for 18 staff
- New product co-ordinator
- Bonus/promotional activity (preparation and monitoring)
- Wholesaler and representative support   (18 representatives nationally)
- Market trends/competitors/general trade activity - reporting
- Product analysis - turnover (individual and brand)
- Pharmacy support programme- data base contact; co-ordination; maintenance; development
- Advertising programme co-ordination; maintenance; support to participants

Achievement:
Promoted to National Marketing Manager based on development and implementation of innovative marketing strategies that increased turnover by 33% in 12 months.

Fig. 11.6 'After' version of the Makeover with Key Words highlighted (page 2)

Selection Criteria Statement (Key Capability Statement) for this role:

SARAH SAMPLE | Key Capabilities Statement

Somewhere, QLD 4223   Email: sarah.sample@gmail.com   Phone: 0000 000 000

Administrative Officer (Generic)   SER227602/16

Key Capability 1: Supports strategic direction

Demonstrated knowledge or ability to rapidly acquire knowledge of departmental administrative policies, practices and procedures used in schools, including relevant student and financial software/programs.

I have 25 years experience in diverse industries where I have consistently supported the strategic direction of each organisation where I was employed.

I have recently completed and passed all 17 units of *Certificate III in Education Support* and have an up-to-date understanding of administrative policies, practices and procedures used in schools. Whilst I have not used any school software programs, I have quickly learned other specialist software programs in my former roles in finance, hospitality, training and legal and accounting services. These included MYOB, Starfleet, EzyRez and Navision. When I commenced my accounts/payroll role at Cullen Bay Resorts they were in the process of changing software programs. Accordingly, I had to learn both programs simultaneously and quickly in order fulfil my role.

In my role as Administrative Assistant at IS Australia in Darwin, I assisted in the preparation of documentation relating to training, policies and strategies that complied with the Australian Training Framework (ATF) and supported the organisation's strategic direction.

I believe these examples demonstrate how I have positively supported strategic direction in previous positions.

Key Capability 2: Achieves results

Demonstrated administrative, keyboard and word processing skills and an ability to work independently and/or with limited supervision.

I possess 25 years' experience in various administrative roles including reception, legal secretary, personal assistant and accounts payable and receivable. I have worked as part of a team and also in situations where I was the only administrative member of staff.

I've completed an advanced secretarial course and am proficient in all areas of administration. When last tested, my typing speed was 75wpm with 100% accuracy.

An example of how I have achieved results for previous organisations is in my role at ABC Resorts. When I joined them, they were in debt for $200,000. I introduced new systems and worked closely with clients in debt, working out payment plans. The result was zero debt when I left.

Another example of my ability to achieve results is in my role of Personal Assistant to the Sales and Marketing Manager at Kendall Australasia. Based on the outstanding results I achieved and my ability to develop and maintain strong relationships with clients and customers, I was promoted to National Marketing Coordinator.

Fig. 11.7 Selection Criteria Statement for Administrative Assistant role page 1

Key Capability 3: Supports productive working relationships

Ability to build and sustain positive working relationships while providing prompt and courteous service to clients.

I enjoy establishing good working relationships with both colleagues and clients and am able to get along with all personalities. I am passionate about providing exceptional customer service and am always willing to go the extra mile to assist clients or solve problems. I make a point of remembering personal details about each client in order to make them feel valued. An example of this is in my cleaning business, where I have worked with a wide range of clients. One of these clients has an adult daughter with a dual disability that makes her fearful of new people in the home. I have developed a very close relationship with this young woman and her family and her mother has offered to be a referee for this application.

Over the last few years in my voluntary role as a support reading and maths tutor at Currumbin State School where my children attend, and also whilst doing my vocational placement for my Certificate III in Education Support, I have developed strong working relationships with the teachers in the classes I assist. Two of these teachers have offered to be my referees.

Key Capability 4: Displays personal drive and integrity

Basic understanding of occupational health and safety, equal employment opportunity and anti-discriminatory practices and behaviour as applied in a work environment.

I have attended numerous OHS training programs and believe that OH&S legislation places the responsibility on both employers and employees at a workplace to ensure the health and safety of others. Employers are responsible for practical procedures that identify and manage exposure to risk in the workplace while employees must follow organisational policies and procedures for the safety of themselves and others.

When I relocated to Darwin, I accepted a short term contract with the government department *NT Power and Water*. Occupational Health and Safety was paramount to the organisation and I attended and recorded minutes of weekly meetings regarding these practices. Also, these topics were covered in great detail in the Education Support course I have recently completed.

I understand that the Equal Employment Opportunity (EEO) Act 1997 ensures that employees are recruited, selected and promoted on an equitable basis. EEO is based on merit based selection because it requires employees to be selected and promoted on the basis of their individual skills and abilities in relation to the requirements of the job and not on personal characteristics such as gender, age, race or nationality.

In all of my roles over the last 25 years, I have worked harmoniously with people from a range of ethnic backgrounds. I enjoy diversity and learn from everyone I meet. I also have utter respect for their individual beliefs and practices and abhor discrimination of any kind.

Key Capability 5: Communicates with influence

Demonstrated interpersonal and communication skills including the ability to work with all members of the school community both individually and as a member of a team.

In all of my former roles, I have demonstrated my ability to work as a member of a harmonious team and also to work independently to achieve organisational objectives. I am a 'people' person and love nothing more than working in a cohesive team to achieve corporate objectives. I've successfully worked independently in roles as a PA and Administration Assistant. My referees will verify my success in both team and independent roles.

My interpersonal and communication skills are shown through receptionist and liaison roles where I have built strong working relationships with clients, management and stakeholders.

Fig. 11.8 Selection Criteria Statement for Administrative Assistant role page 2

SARAH SAMPLE

Somewhere, QLD 4223   Email: sarah.sample@gmail.com   Phone: 0000 000 000

Administrative Officer (Generic)   SER227602/16

Key Capability 1: Supports strategic direction

Demonstrated knowledge or ability to rapidly acquire knowledge of departmental administrative policies, practices and procedures used in schools, including relevant student and financial software/programs.

I have 25 years' experience in diverse industries where I have consistently supported the strategic direction of each organisation where I was employed.

I have recently completed and passed all 17 units of *Certificate III in Education Support* and have an up-to-date understanding of administrative policies, practices and procedures used in schools. Whilst I have not used any school software programs, I have quickly learned other specialist software programs in my former roles in finance, hospitality, training and legal and accounting services. These included MYOB, Starfleet, EzyRez and Navision. When I commenced my accounts/payroll role at ABC Resorts, they were in the process of changing software programs. Accordingly, I had to learn both programs simultaneously and quickly in order to fulfil my role. I was up and running in a matter of days.

In my role as Administrative Assistant at IST Australia in Darwin, I assisted in the preparation of documentation relating to training, policies and strategies that complied with the Australian Training Framework (ATF) and supported the organisation's strategic direction.

I believe these examples demonstrate how I have positively supported strategic direction in previous positions.

Key Capability 2: Achieves results

Demonstrated administrative, keyboard and word processing skills and an ability to work independently and/or with limited supervision.

I possess 25 years' experience in various administrative roles including reception, legal secretary, personal assistant and accounts payable and receivable. I have worked as part of a team and also in situations where I was the only administrative member of staff.

I've completed an advanced secretarial course and am proficient in all areas of administration. When last tested, my typing speed was 75wpm with 100% accuracy.

An example of how I have achieved results for previous organisations is in my role at ABC Resorts. When I joined them, they were in debt for $200,000. I introduced new systems and worked closely with clients in debt, working out payment plans. The result was zero debt when I left.

Another example of my ability to achieve results is in my role of Personal Assistant to the Sales and Marketing Manager at ABC Australasia. Based on the outstanding results I achieved and my ability to develop and maintain strong relationships with clients and customers, I was promoted to National Marketing Coordinator.

I am confident that the above examples show my ability to consistently achieve results for the organisation.

Fig. 11.9 Key Capability Statement with key words shown page 1

Somewhere, QLD 4223   Email: sarah.sample@gmail.com   Phone: 0000 000 000

Key Capability 3: Supports productive working relationships

Ability to build and sustain positive working relationships while providing prompt and courteous service to clients.

I enjoy establishing good working relationships with both colleagues and clients and am able to get along with all personalities. I am passionate about providing exceptional customer service and am always willing to go the extra mile to assist clients or solve problems. I make a point of remembering personal details about each client in order to make them feel valued. I have received numerous recommendations from clients about my customer service.

Over the last few years in my voluntary role as a support reading and maths tutor at ABC State School where my children attend, and also whilst doing my vocational placement for the Certificate III in Education Support course, I have developed strong working relationships with the teachers in the classes where I assist. Two of these teachers have offered to be my referees which demonstrates their confidence in my abilities.

Key Capability 4: Displays personal drive and integrity

Basic understanding of occupational health and safety, equal employment opportunity and anti-discriminatory practices and behaviour as applied in a work environment.

I have attended numerous OH&S training programs and believe that OH&S legislation places the responsibility on both employers and employees at a workplace to ensure the health and safety of others. Employers are responsible for practical procedures that identify and manage exposure to risk in the workplace while employees must follow organisational policies and procedures for the safety of themselves and others.

I understand that the Equal Employment Opportunity (EEO) Act 1997 ensures that employees are recruited, selected and promoted on an equitable basis. EEO is based on merit based selection because it requires employees to be selected and promoted on the basis of their individual skills and abilities in relation to the requirements of the job and not on personal characteristics such as gender, age, race or nationality.

In all of my roles over the last 25 years, I have worked harmoniously with people from a range of ethnic backgrounds. I enjoy diversity and learn from everyone I meet. I also respect their individual beliefs and practices and abhor any discriminatory practices.

Key Capability 5: Communicates with influence

Demonstrated interpersonal and communication skills including the ability to work with all members of the school community both individually and as a member of a team.

In all of my former roles, I have demonstrated my ability to work as a member of a harmonious team and also to work independently to achieve organisational objectives. I am a 'people' person and love nothing more than working in a cohesive team to achieve corporate objectives. I've successfully worked independently in roles as a PA and Administration Assistant. My referees will verify my success in both team and independent roles.

My interpersonal and communication skills are shown through frontline receptionist and liaison roles where I have built strong working relationships with clients, management and stakeholders.

I am confident that I have demonstrated my ability to communicate with influence in all of my former roles.

Fig. 11.10 Key Capability Statement with key words shown page 2

Chapter 12

Where to from here?

Hopefully, you're fired up and ready to take on the world with your updated résumé, cover letter and LinkedIn Profile. Your next career is just around the corner.

Make sure you use LinkedIn and other social media to network with former colleagues, management, suppliers and clients – you never know when they will have an opportunity to offer you. Keep active on LinkedIn and offer endorsements for friends and colleagues. In turn, ask them to write endorsements for you also.

Keep all documents from applications you've written so you can review them and learn from them. They will make your next application much faster to prepare.

To be competitive, you need to keep up-to-the-minute with your professional development. Deakin University in Victoria offers some fantastic FREE online courses to help career changers. Check their website regularly to see what's coming up.

Learning how to 'sell' yourself is a very valuable skill and now you can take a free three week online course to build your confidence. This course is a free introduction to a unique Deakin University postgraduate degree: Master of Professional Practice, that allows you to earn credentials based on your industry experience.

The course is aimed at professionals who are considering a career change. It will be particularly appealing to mid-career professionals looking to plan their next step.

Here are the details of the course:
https://www.futurelearn.com/courses/career-smart-sell-yourself

Course Name: Becoming Career Smart: How to Sell Yourself

Thinking about your next career steps? Identify your key strengths and skills, and learn how to sell them and yourself. This course is designed for anyone applying for jobs or courses. It will be of particular interest to those in the early stages of their career, or those who are out of practice and need to update their skills. No prior knowledge or expertise is needed.

Following in the Resources for Career Changers are Templates, Examples, Cheat Sheets and Checklists to help you hit the deck running with your applications.

Good luck with your new career!

Celebrate your career success –
your life, your actions...
that lead to a brilliant career launch!

Patience, persistence and perspiration

make un unbeatable

combination for success.

Napolean Hill

The foundation stones for a balanced

success are honesty, character,

integrity, faith, love and loyalty.

Zig Ziglar

It had long since come to my attention

that people of accomplishment rarely

sat back and let things happen to them.

They went out and happened to things.

Leonardo da Vinci

Success is how you bounce

when you hit rock bottom.

George S. Patton

Testimonials

'I've been unemployed for 18 months, sending off dozens of applications every week without getting a single reply. I spent the weekend updating my Résumé and sent off a very tailored application...and got an interview 2 days later. I can't believe how quickly my new résumé got results. It really works. Thanks.'

Andrew Wood

'I've been trying to get a book keeping job for 6 months – without any luck. I didn't know about 'robots' and 'key words' or what they would have to do with book keeping. I followed the steps in the book and have an interview next week. That's amazing! I feel much more confident since reading this book. Thank you.'

Jan Smith

'I'm fifty-three years old and can't afford to 'retire' as my former boss suggested when I was retrenched. The mortgage won't pay itself off so I have to get a job. This little book showed me where I was going wrong...everywhere. I was using a résumé that worked ten years ago but isn't working now. It's a whole new ball game. I even have a LinkedIn profile now. I've just applied for three great jobs – wouldn't it be hilarious if I got all three? I'll let you know.'

Lucinda Wright

'What do you do when you've had your own business for 30 years and then get an offer to buy you out? I wasn't in a strong financial position so I couldn't retire. I gave my résumé a makeover as per this book and decided to bite the bullet and send off some applications – one of them was for a train driver position with VIC Rail. I was thrilled when I passed the first round of the process, so obviously my résumé worked. Unfortunately, I missed out on the next round where only 20 of over 2,000 applicants were selected for training. I'm confident to apply for another job after this experience.'

James Sutton

Resources for Career Changers, Templates and Figures

To access the TEMPLATES, QUICKGUIDES, CHEAT SHEETS and DOWNLOADABLE FIGURES FROM THE BOOK, please go to:

http://smartstartmarketingsolutions.com.au/members

The login credentials are:

User: member

Password: SmartMarketing2017

Cheat Sheet
Homonym List

Quick Guides
Proofreading

Formatting

Linked Profile

Templates
Administration Officer Résumé

Administration Officer Cover Letter

Administration Officer Key Capabilities Statement

Business Development Manager Résumé

Marketing and Communication Manager Résumé

Senior Project Manager Résumé

Modern Multi-Role Résumé

How to use the templates in this book

There are an abundance of résumé templates online that look very attractive with colours, boxes, fancy fonts, photos and other formatting enhancements.

Unfortunately, some Applicant Tracking Systems (ATS) will not be able to recognise these elements and your résumé may look like gobbledegook. It's better to be safe than sorry – don't touch them.

The Word templates that come with this book are ATS-Friendly and have been tested on several ATS scanners. They use the KISS Principle – Keep It Simple Sweetheart!

If you prefer, you can do your own formatting using our generic templates with helpful guides.

The resume templates with this book are very easy to use. Open up a few to choose the layout you prefer. The Communication and Marketing Manager Template is suitable for most roles. Or, if you are a Project Manager or IT professional, choose the Senior Project Manager Template. It allows for scope of projects to be listed in a slightly different format.

 Simply copy the template to your computer. Change the name of the file to 'yourname_position' and save the document. Now, all you have to do is replace the text that is already there with your own information. We just tested the Marketing and Communication Manager Template and it took 40 minutes to write a resume from scratch by just replacing the text. Of course, you will be doing a lot of work analysing the PD, and identifying and using key words, so it will take you longer to prepare your materials. Once you have this done, the actual resume won't take long to complete.

The formatting is already done for you, so that saves you heaps of time.

Remember to update the *Properties* section of your document to add to your key words. To do this, click the *Office Button* in the top left hand side of the page. Choose *Prepare*, then choose *Properties*. Update this section with your name as the author and provide key words from the Position Description. This metadata will add to the key words in your applications. If you don't do this, you will have my name as the author on your metadata.

Good luck with your job applications. Please send feedback on how you found the book – was it helpful? Did it solve a problem you had with getting to an interview?

Please send your thoughts to: dawn@ssms.com.au

Other books by this author

Get That Government Job (2e): The secrets to winning applications with selection criteria

Purchase at: http://smartstartmarketing.com.au/government-job/

Selection Criteria Toolkit: How to 'sell' yourself with a winner application ... and nail that job

Purchase at: http://smartstartmarketing.com.au/product/selection-criteria-toolkit/

From Fired to Hired: The Quick and Easy Job Guide for Baby Boomers

Purchase at: http://smartstartmarketing.com.au/fired-to-hired/

Made in the USA
Columbia, SC
18 August 2017